Junior Gymnastics

Peter Aykroyd

Macdonald

Contents

Editorial manager
Chester Fisher
Editor
Linda Sonntag
Designer
Peter Benoist
Production
Penny Kitchenham

First published 1980
Macdonald Educational Ltd
Holywell House
Worship Street
London EC2A 2EN

Printed and bound by
Purnell & Sons Limited
Paulton (Bristol) and London
ISBN paperback 0 356 06791 2
hardback 0 356 06792 0

The editor wishes to thank Peter Benoist for his invaluable help and technical advice.

Introduction

One of the leading Soviet gymnasts of the 70s, Alexandre Detiatin, dismounts from the high bar on to a crash mat.

Many people believe, and you may, too, that gymnastics is very new in origin. Why? Because it is a sport which is exactly in tune with our modern age. It is exciting to perform and fascinating to watch. And gymnastics provides a challenge for the individual—individual because you don't have to be a member of a team as in football or have an opponent to play as in squash.

Gymnastics has other worthwhile qualities, too. It uses many natural movements of the body in different ways so that most of your muscles are exercised. That is why gymnasts are among the fittest of all sportsmen and women. These natural movements also link gymnastics with art and bring an important element of grace to its performance.

However modern gymnastics may seem, its beginnings go back in time for thousands of years. The ancient Greeks and Romans made good use of physical exercises and the early Olympic Games held in Greece featured many gymnastics activities. After the Greek and Roman ages, few people performed gymnastics in any form except for tumblers, jousters and dancers during the Middle Ages. Its rebirth during the 18th and 19th centuries was linked to the development in Europe of large professional armies to whom physical fitness became an important part of training. Two educationalists at this time were a great influence on modern gymnastics: Pehr Henrik Ling (1776-1839) of Sweden and Friederich Ludwig Jahn of Germany (1778-1839. Ling was concerned with free physical expression as being vital to education while Jahn established some of the fixed apparatus used today—the rings, the horse, the parallel bars and the horizontal bar.

The first gymnastics club in the USA was started in 1850 while the International Gymnastics Federation (FIG), the sport's international governing body, was formed in 1881. The British Amateur Gymnastics Association, which controls the sport in Britain, was founded in 1888. When the Modern Olympic Games began in 1896, one of the seven sports included was gymnastics which was performed almost entirely by teams of men. Women gymnasts first took part in the Olympics in 1928. The first world championships, now held in the year before and after each Olympic Games, were held in 1934 and the World Cup, a major annual event, was established in 1975.

From 1960, world-wide television coverage began to increase the popularity of gymnastics and it was television at the 1972 Munich Olympic Games which presented the unforgettable Olga Korbut, then aged 17, to a huge international audience of

Nadia Comaneci of Romania shows on the beam the qualities of precision and daring which made her an international champion.

millions. It was the young Soviet star's personality, not her achievements, which began the boom in gymnastics during the 1970s.

Olga was eclipsed at the 1976 Olympic Games in Montreal by a Romanian gymnast of almost unbelievable artistry. She was Nadia Comaneci, aged 14, who was given a perfect score of ten not once but seven times.

If you have your heart set on becoming a successful gymnast or entering top competitions such as the Thames Television Junior Gymnast of the Year competition, then this book will show you many of the skills and techniques which you will need to acquire. First, you must become a member of a gym club. Your school may run one, or there may be one in your neighbourhood. Many clubs are full, so you may have to wait before you can join. You may also have to have a test to see if your body is in good enough shape to undergo gymnastics training. Once you are a member of a gym club, your progress is up to you. There is no easy way to the top. It takes hard work, but with the right attitude and knowledge, you can enjoy every moment of your training and the competitions that you enter.

Kathy Williams, a schoolgirl from Manchester, is an up-and-coming British gymnast (above).

A sideways splits on the beam performed by leading American gymnast Kathy Johnson (below).

Preparation

Every famous gymnast started off the same way. He or she spent a great deal of time on preparing muscles for gymnastics and learning basic skills.

The six apparatus pieces for men—floor, pommelled horse, rings, vault, parallel bars and high bar—and the four for women—vault, asymmetric bars, balance beam and floor—are designed to make gymnasts show many abilities. So it makes good sense to learn the basics of gymnastics thoroughly.

You will then find that you can tackle difficult moves and routines with confidence and style. If you attempt advanced gymnastics too soon, the outcome will be that you obtain poor results in competitions. So what qualities should you as a young gymnast have and what should you aim to achieve in body preparation?

Leading gymnastics coaches look out for boys and girls with the right build. A gymnast should be slim in figure and upright in posture. The strength-weight ratio must be right, too, for example, it is a disadvantage to have a heavy body and short arms, as the arms would have to acquire considerable strength. It helps to have long fingers as well in order to grasp bars.

With the right build must come speed of action, ability to spring in the air and, for girls, a strong sense of rhythm and balance. And all gymnasts must have the natural ability of co-ordination which is combining movements of the limbs.

Some mental qualities are vital as well. The ideal gymnast will be able to concentrate and think quickly during routines. Some moves have an element of danger about them; bravery is certainly needed here. Above all, the ideal gymnast is determined enough to face adversities such as injury or loss of form without becoming discouraged.

In body preparation, you must aim for:

Suppleness to achieve the maximum range of movement

Strength to enable you to perform many movements

Body tension to tighten muscles in your back, stomach, legs and seat so that they do not sag during certain moves

Stamina to let you perform without becoming tired quickly

Barry Winch, a British international, demonstrates a straddle support on one bar of the parallel bars.

Twisting as he dismounts from the parallel bars is Alexandre Detiatin of the USSR, a consistently good performer.

British champion Susan Cheesebrough shows first-class leg extension as she performs on the beam.

If you can achieve these qualities, you are well on the way to becoming a good gymnast. Your gym club should help you become sufficiently prepared for serious training.

Safety
In the gym, it is common sense to make sure that all training is as safe as possible. So for safety's sake, here are some rules to follow.

1 Pay attention to your coach's instructions.
2 Do not play the fool during training.
3 Never wear anything that may interfere with your hands, your vision, or your coach's vision.
4 Do not wear jewellery—rings, watches, necklaces and so on — when training or performing.
5 If you have to wear glasses, make sure that they are securely fastened.
6 Keep your hands dry at all times with 'chalk'. In gyms, this is magnesium carbonate powder which absorbs sweat thus preventing loss of grip.
7 Do not train unless a qualified coach or teacher is there.
8 Do not train if you do not feel well.

Your coach
Many top gymnasts owe their success to their coach. A qualified coach will know a great deal about the sport and can help you reach high standards. So listen carefully if a coach is criticising a move or explaining something such as a routine. Do not waste the coach's time or yours. Try a skill the way the coach tells you and collect as many coaching tips as you can. A good idea is to keep a notebook so that you can write ideas down. If you wish to change a movement in a routine, you should ask your coach.

Remember, a coach puts a great deal of effort into the training of a gymnast and it is only fair that the gymnast co-operates with the training set by the coach or the club.

Your clothing
Clothing for gymnastics should be light and fit well. In training, nothing loose should be worn which could catch in any apparatus or hinder your vision. You should never wear a belt with a buckle. All clothing must be clean and tidy.

Track suits Track suits protect your arms and legs from abrasions during training and keep you warm. Your club may have its own style of track suit for its members.

Leotards These one-piece costumes are named after a French acrobat of the last century. They should not be too tight or too baggy. Girls should not let their pants or knickers be visible: this

This exercise may take you some time to achieve—so keep trying!

The immortal Olga Korbut completes the somersault named after her on the high bar of the asymmetric bars.

Edward Azarian (USSR), son of famous gymnast Albert, is at ease on pommels (left).

One of the best performers on the high bar in the West is Eberhard Gienger, West Germany (right).

Emilia Eberle is another Romanian gymnast who is making her name known internationally (below).

makes a bad impression during performances. Again, your club may have its own special leotard.
Shoes The best footwear by far is gymnastic slippers which are light with thin soles. Do not let the soles become too worn as this might cause you to slip. You could also slip if you performed in socks. If you are ordering gymnastics slippers by mail, send a piece of paper with the outline of your feet drawn on it.
White trousers These are worn by men during performances on all disciplines except for floor and vault when shorts are usually worn. Trousers must not only fit well and allow complete freedom of movement but also stand up to strenuous activity.

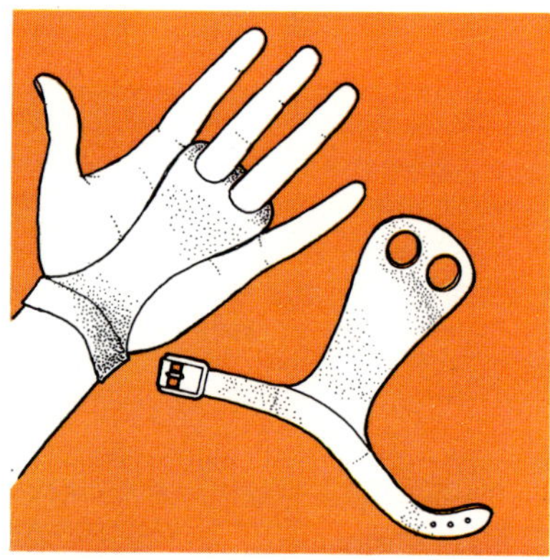

Handguards Handguards protect the palms of gymnasts' hands when they work on the pommelled horse, rings, parallel bars, high bar and asymmetric bars. Handguards come in different materials such as leather or lamp wick. They are worn by placing the two middle fingers in the holes and buckling the strap around the wrist. Make sure that your handguards fit comfortably and tightly with your hands in a cupped position. The rough surface of the handguards should be in contact with the apparatus. Remember to check your handguards regularly for wear. Do not perform in them if they have slippery surfaces or are torn.

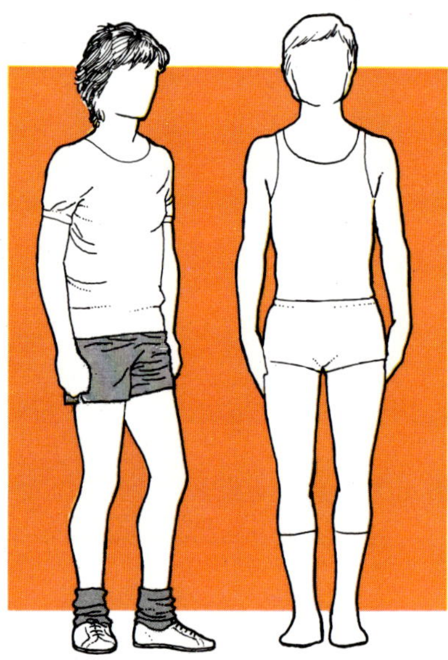

Tidy, healthy gymnasts make the best impressions on judges.

Body care

Gymnasts who take care of their health and appearance have a big advantage in competitions over those who look slovenly and ungroomed. Here are a few hints to help you look and feel your best.
Hair Keep it neat. Don't let it cover your eyes. Girls with long hair must tie it back during training and competitions.
Hands Take extra care of your hands—they are vital to you in gymnastics. Keep the palms moist with daily use of hand lotion or vaseline but not before training.
Exercise Try and carry out some form of exercise at home on days when you are not training in the gym. The simplest exercise of all is jogging.
Diet As a gymnast, you use a great deal of energy. This must be replaced by eating foods containing the energy nutrients of carbohydrates, proteins and fats. Bread and potatoes, for example, are carbohydrate foods, cheese and butter are among those which contain fats, and protein is found in foods such as meat and milk. So make sure you eat a good balanced diet every day.

Preventing injury

Gymnastics is a sport which has its full share of sprains and strains and a well-run gym club will have a first-aid kit at hand to treat injuries. Here are some points about injury to remember.

1 Report any injury however minor to your coach. Immediate treatment may help it heal quickly.

2 Do not resume training until you have fully recovered from a painful injury. Otherwise that injury may take even longer to heal.

3 A tip for girls: use vinyl foam to protect your hips from bruising when training on the asymmetric bars. Vinyl foam can also be used to pad the vertebrae of the neck when you practise rolls on the beam.

4 Do not let callouses build up on your hands. Callouses can be torn off during apparatus work—painfully. So 'file' them down with a pumice stone or emery board.

Warm up

One of the most important rules of gymnastics is to warm up at the start of every training session or competition.

You should not spend less than 20 minutes on your warm-up and you should aim to exercise all parts of your body. During your warm-up, you should wear warm clothing such as a track suit to help raise your body temperature quickly.

When you have finished your warm-up, all your muscles should have been stretched and relaxed. Only then are you ready to start training.

On the next page are some examples of warm-up exercises. You should perform the easiest ones first. At some gym clubs, the gymnasts warm up to music, which makes the warm-up period more fun.

1 Warming all muscles
Running and skipping on the spot or around the gym will warm and loosen all your muscles. It will also exercise your heart. This is a good way to start your warm-up.

2 Feet and ankles
Stand on tip-toes and jump several times high in the air, landing lightly. This exercise will strengthen your feet and ankles and help you improve your 'spring'.

3 Shoulders
To give flexibility to your shoulders, stretch and swing your arms forwards, sideways and upwards. Repeat for at least half a minute.

4 Waist
Your waist muscles will benefit from this stretch exercise. Reach up with your arms and press your body and head over to the right four times and then do the same on the left. Do not bend forward at the waist.

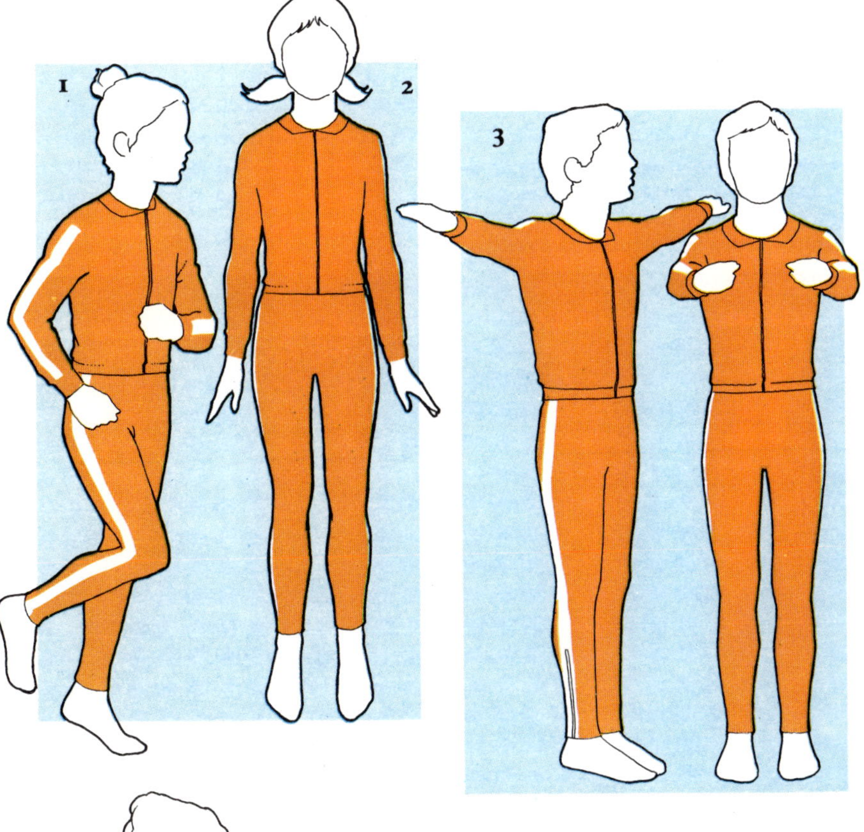

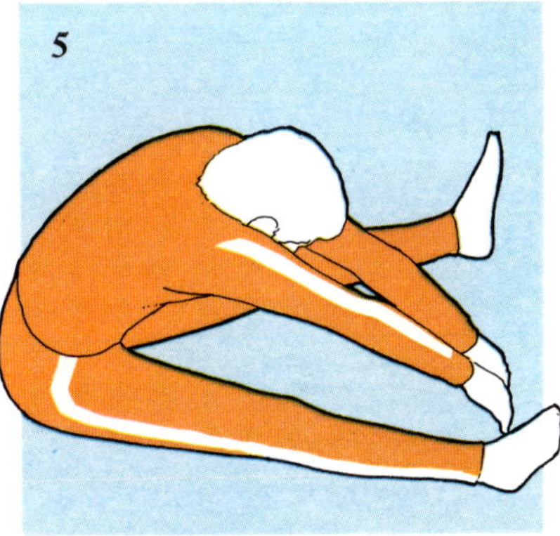

5 Legs
This will help you make your leg muscles supple. Bend from your waist forward slowly with your head down. You should aim to touch the floor without bouncing.

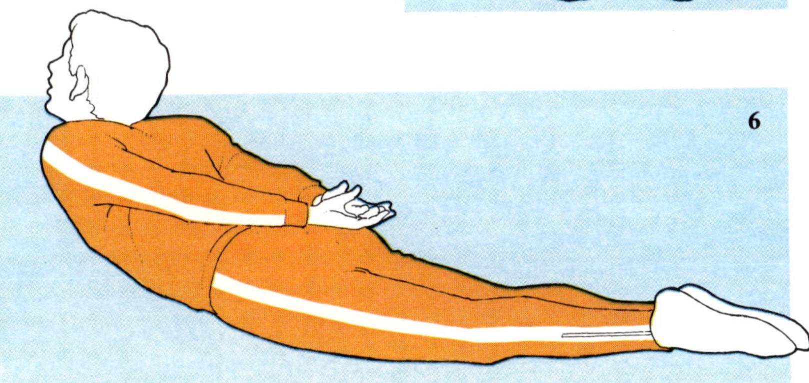

6 Back and tummy
Here is an exercise which is excellent for your tummy and lower back muscles as well as helping to improve body tension. Lie on your tummy and link your thumbs behind your back. Lift your head and chest, trying to keep your feet on the floor. Hold, lower and repeat.

Anatomy of the vault

Many gymnasts use the word 'explosive' when they talk about vaulting. For both men and women gymnasts, this event calls for a burst of speed, a vigorous jump and a steady landing—all over in a few seconds.

The horse—the piece of equipment which gymnasts vault over—has its origins in the wooden horses used many many years ago by Greek and Roman warriors. Wooden horses were used to teach soldiers how to mount and dismount and they remained an important training item over the centuries when knights in armour went into battle on horses.

In the early 19th century, when modern gymnastics began to develop, the wooden horse was already in use. About this time, the tradition of jumping on to the horse was replaced by the practice of jumping or vaulting over it. Vaulting over the leather-topped box or horse became a feature of physical education in many countries.

Men vault over the horse lengthways on while women tackle it sideways. These two positions are known as the *long horse* and the *broad horse*.

Vaulting, in common with the other gymnastics apparatus, is marked out of a maximum of ten points. Vaults, however, vary in difficulty and thus in rating. The International Gymnastics Federation (FIG) publishes lists of ratings for apparatus in the *Code of Points*.

The system of scoring for men differs from that for women, so the *Code of Points* is set out in two books: one for men and one for women. Both books lay down working regulations and show how judges deduct points in competitions.

Parts of the vault

All vaults have six parts, all of which are important because the success of each part depends on how well you perform the preceding part.

In learning these stages of vaulting, both boys and girls follow the same basic sequence. Later, when you tackle the more advanced vaults, the stages have to be adapted.

The parts are: run-up, take-off, flight on, thrust, flight off, and landing.

On the right is a diagram of a girl's handspring vault showing the six parts.

Here is the moment before the thrust which will take the gymnast into a high, short flight-off for a Yamashita vault.

Run-up

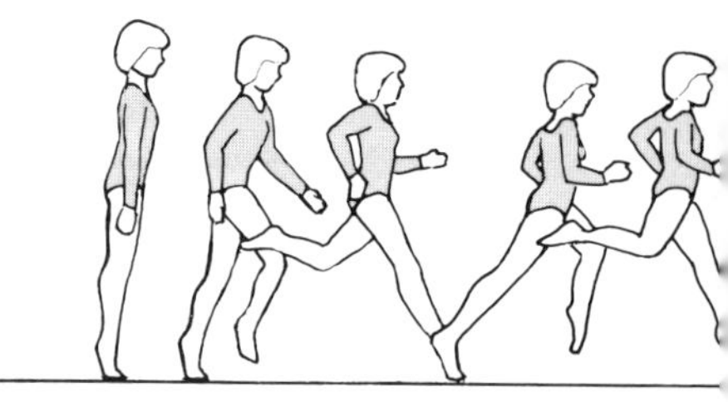

Run-up
FIG rules say that the run-up for men must be a maximum of 20 metres. For women, it should be at least 15 metres. Start your run slowly and increase your speed so that you reach your fastest at the springboard. Jump onto the springboard with feet together and arms back.

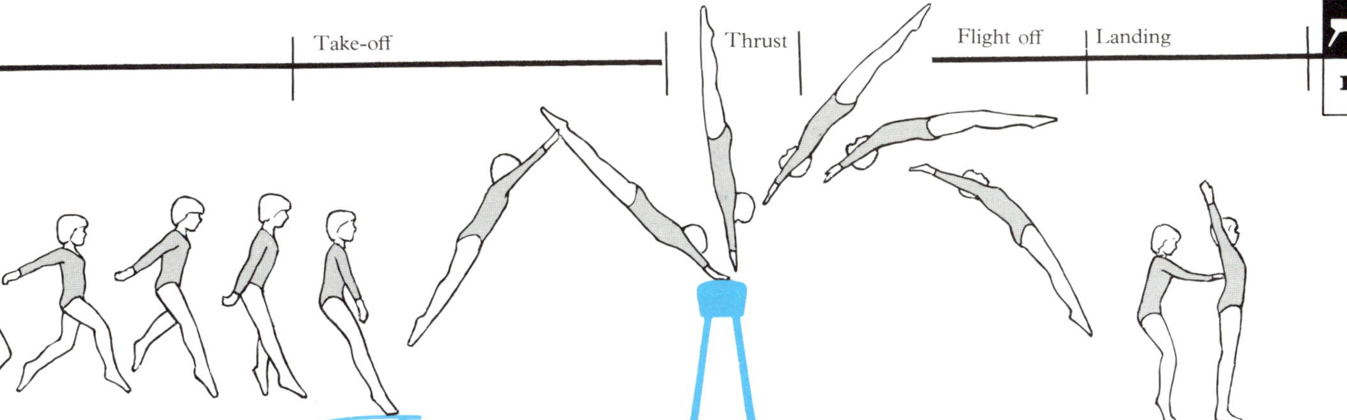

Take-off
Your feet should land on the springboard ahead of your hips but they should not leave the springboard until your body weight is in front of them. So swing your arms quickly forwards and upwards and *jump*, obtaining maximum stretch from your legs and ankles as well.

Flight on
Aim for a short, fast flight onto the horse. Otherwise you will find it difficult to obtain a long, high flight off.

Thrust
You should touch the horse with straight arms before your body is upright. Then push up with your wrists and shoulders.

Flight off
Try to cover as much height and distance as possible.

Landing
Keep feet and knees together, with knees slightly bent.

Olga Koval of the Soviet Union thrusts off before she completes a tucked Tsukahara vault in competition.

Elena Davydova (USSR) holds a tucked position in her flight off as she rotates towards her landing.

The apparatus
Measurements and specifications for all gymnastics apparatus including the vaulting horse are determined by the FIG and must be followed in all major competitions.

The springboard
The springboard, which is vital to vaulting, is used by both men and women. It can also be used for the asymmetric bars and balance beam according to rules in the *Code of Points*. While the measurements of the springboard are fixed, the distance it has to be from the horse is not. This distance depends on the ability and experience of the gymnast. Top gymnasts rarely have the springboard further than their own height away from the horse.

The horse
Men As mentioned, men vault with the horse lengthways on. The height of the horse is set at 1.35 metres. There are two touching zones each taking up one half of the horse — the croup (near half) and the neck (far half). During his vault the gymnast must put his hands on either the croup or the neck (but not between them) and this can affect the vault's tariff. For example, the rating of a Yamashita vault performed on the neck is 9.0 points. On the croup, it is valued at 9.4. In a competition, men perform one vault.
Women The horse for women's vaulting is positioned broadways with its height at 1.10 metres. In their competitions, women perform two vaults and score with the better of the two. As women have no set measurement of run-up, they should aim to find a personal length of run which will allow them to reach maximum speed as soon as possible.

Training
Training for vaulting should first centre around the six parts of a vault. Once you are a competent vaulter, your training—apart from learning new vaults—can concentrate on improving your vaulting muscles. This means performing regular exercises for legs and ankles such as skipping with a rope, skip-jumping holding a weight to your chest, or raising your heels up and down.

The basic exercises shown here will help you understand vaulting and improve the standards of your performance. On the following pages, you will find examples of vaults which can be performed in competition by both boys and girls with the horse positioned accordingly.

Some vaults and gymnastics movements are named after the gymnasts who first performed them. Two such famous vaults are Yamashita and Tsukahara.

Run-up
- You can improve the running action of your arms and legs when you practise sprinting over distances of 20, 30, 40 and 50 metres. Your arms should be bent at the elbows and pump backwards and forwards.
- To develop leg strength and arm swing further, run with a

coach or partner resisting you with his or her arms on your shoulders as he or she runs or walks backwards.

● Place a low object such as a medicine ball or bench in front of the springboard. Run and jump over the object on to the springboard, landing on both feet. This exercise will help you judge the height and length of your jump onto the springboard.

Take-off

● To improve foot action, jump off a bench onto a springboard and then on to a crash mat with your feet together and bending as in the diagram and your arms swinging upwards and forwards.

● Do the same but jump up from the springboard onto a low vaulting box top or bench. Then jump off.

● Jump up and down on the springboard with someone in front of you supporting your arms. This, too, will help leg power and stretch.

● Practise your arm swing by jumping from the springboard to reach up and catch a rope or rings or bar above you. Make sure there is a crash mat there to fall on.

Flight-on

● Play leapfrog and try to take off further and further away from your partner. Place lines on the floor to give you your 'launching pad' position.

● From standing, dive forward, roll on to a crash mat as far as you can. Get some helpers to hold a piece of string low for you to dive

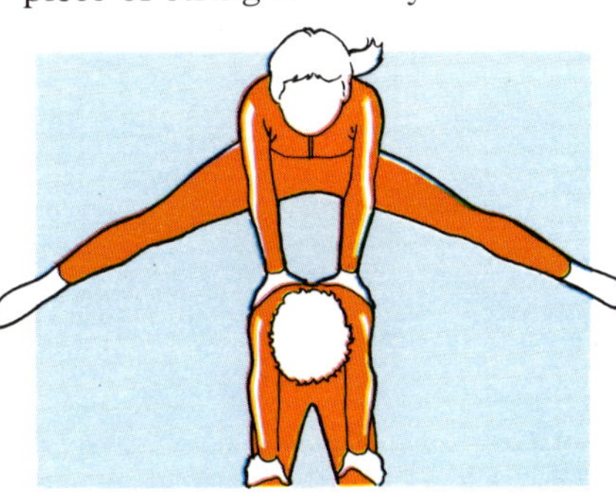

over without touching it.

● Now try the dive roll from a springboard onto two layers of crash mats.

Thrust

● Hold a medicine ball to your chest and thrust it as far as possible.

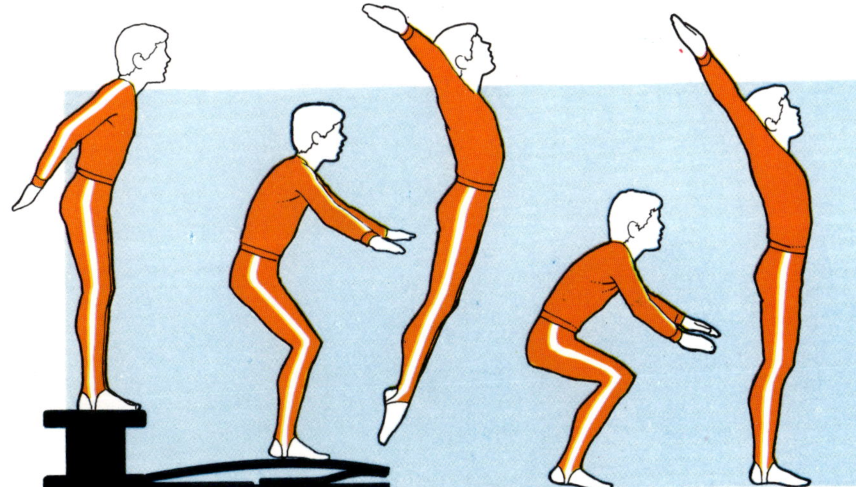

● Jump onto your hands and then push yourself back onto your feet.

● Supporting yourself on your hands, as in performing a press-up, dip your body and then push through your shoulders while lifting your hips and taking your

legs forward past your hands.

● Here, you jump up onto the vaulting horse longways and then, putting your hands on the far end, push off with legs apart to land upright on a crash mat. This exercise should be tried on the floor and then have support for safety when performed on the horse.

Flight-off and landing

● Jump off a low bench with your body, arms and legs stretched. On landing, have a partner push you off balance—slightly. Now adjust your position quickly to regain your balance.

● From a vaulting horse, jump down keeping your body again stretched in the air. Bend your ankles, knees and hips to absorb the shock of landing. Try not to step forwards or backwards. Stand upright quickly.

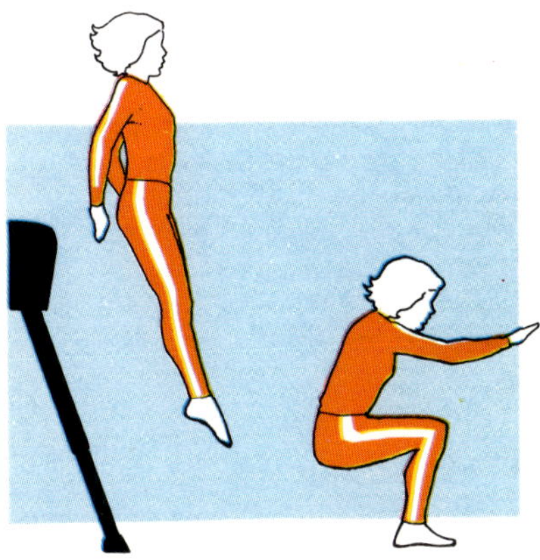

THE STRADDLE

The straddle is another basic vault with the same approach as for the squat. On contact with the horse, start the straddle. Thrust off firmly, lifting your arms, legs and body up. Once clear of the horse, close your legs quickly and straighten to land. Leapfrogging is good practice for this vault.

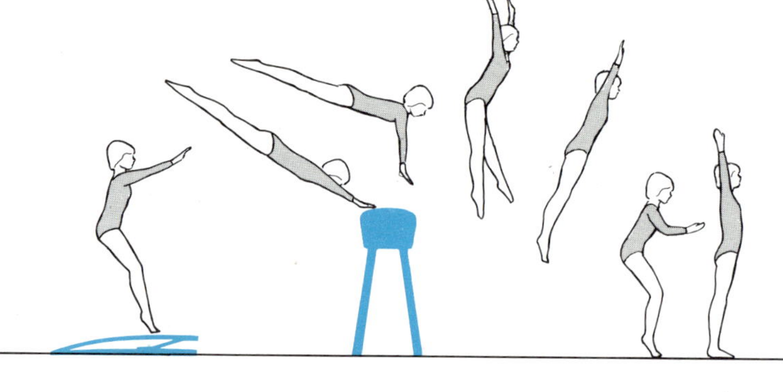

THE SQUAT

This vault is a basic one which all young gymnasts learn. From take-off, reach for the horse with your body almost horizontal. On contact, tuck your knees up to your arms and thrust down strongly with your hands. Over the horse, your legs should not go through your arms but must straighten, once clear of the horse, for the landing.

STOOP

The stoop resembles the squat except that your legs remain straight and pass under your body. In order to do so, your hips have to be high and therefore you need a faster run-up and stronger take-off and thrust.

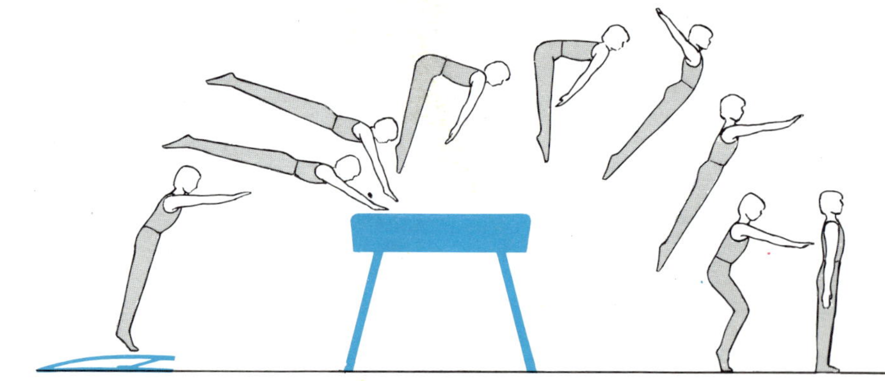

STRADDLE WITH HALF TURN

In this variation of the straddle, the gymnast turns in the flight-off to land facing the horse. This is achieved by bringing the left leg forward and past the right one. The turn is helped further by the hips and the head before the gymnast straightens the whole body for landing.

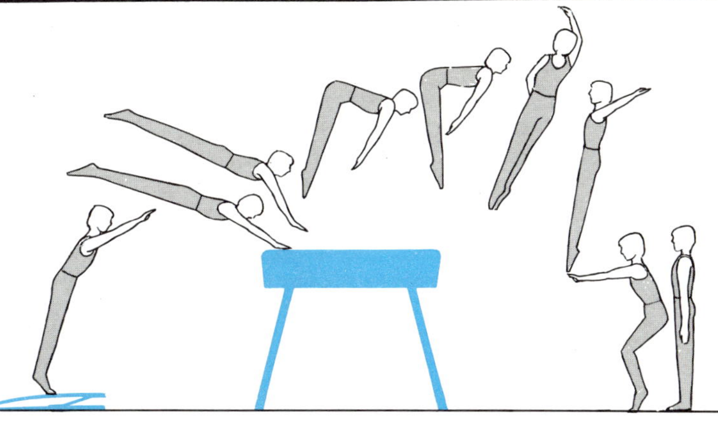

STOOP WITH HALF TURN
With high flight-off, you can vary the sequence of the stoop vault by turning to face the horse on landing. Use your hips, arms and head to execute this half turn.

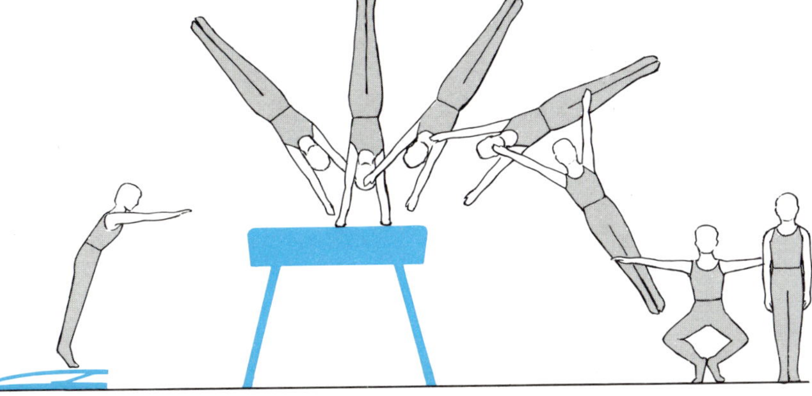

CARTWHEEL
On take-off, you must make a quarter turn. Cartwheel onto your left hand, keeping your legs together. Your left hand is followed by your right hand onto the horse. Thrust off with both hands and land with your body still sideways to the horse. In men's vaulting, this vault is called the Hollander.

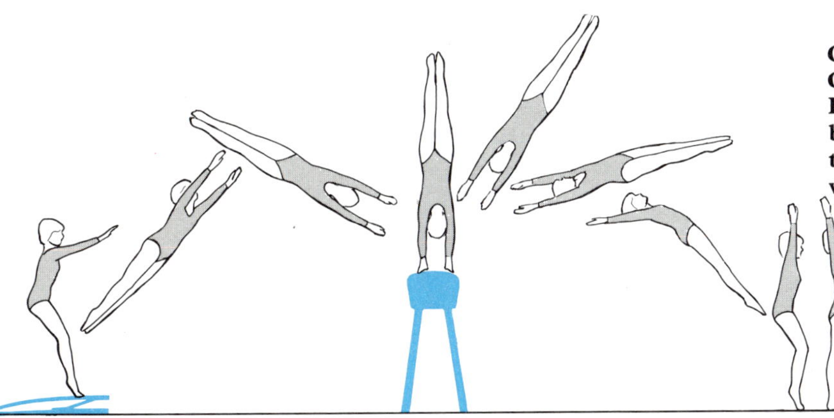

CARTWHEEL WITH QUARTER TURN OUTWARD
Perform the cartwheel as above but revolve your body in a half turn during the flight-off to land with your back to the horse.

CARTWHEEL WITH FULL TURN OUTWARD
This version of the cartwheel, when you complete a full turn in flight-off, has a sideways landing which is tricky to achieve. This is because you have very little time to control your balance and stand upright after landing.

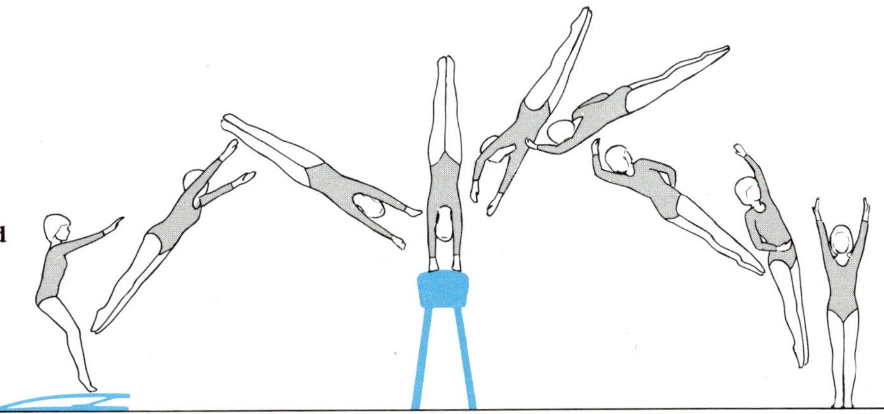

HECHT

The Hecht requires a very strong thrust off the horse. This is to counteract the rotation of your body without lowering your legs while at the same time keeping your body straight. When your arms swing out in the flight-off, it gives the impression of gliding.

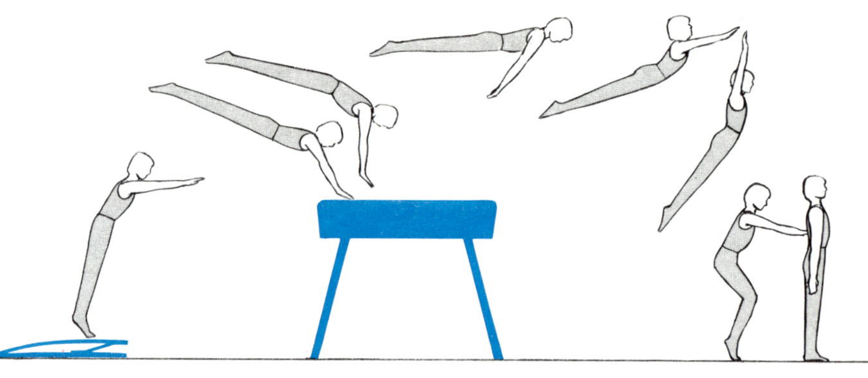

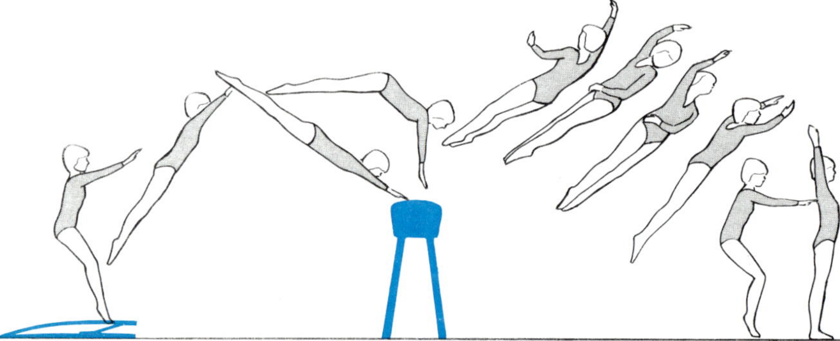

HECHT WITH FULL TURN

In this difficult vault, you have to swing your arms out before making a full turn in the flight-off phase. Again, you will need a very powerful thrust off the horse to master this variation of the Hecht.

HANDSPRING

The handspring is very important, being an advanced vault on which others are based. You need a powerful run-up and take-off to raise your heels quickly while keeping your body straight. Thrust immediately and strongly, still keeping your body straight as it rotates for the landing.

HANDSPRING WITH HALF TURN

In making a half turn during the flight-off of the handspring, remember to keep your body straight. Take care, too, not to step backwards.

HANDSPRING WITH FULL TURN
The ingredients are the same: you must perform a powerful run, an explosive take-off, and a strong thrust to obtain a successful full turn on this highly-rated vault.

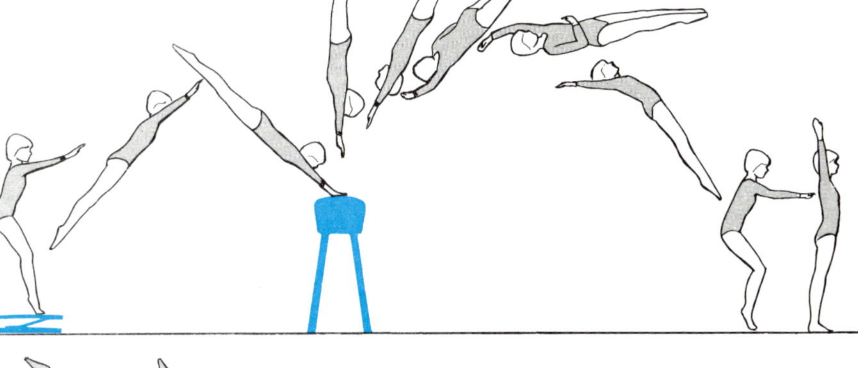

YAMASHITA
The Yamashita is a handspring vault with the gymnast holding a tight piked position in the flight-off. The flight-on has a flatter flight than the handspring, the flight-off being higher and shorter. The thrust must take your body and arms up towards the feet into the pike.

TSUKAHARA TUCKED
The flight-on of the Tsukahara is a cartwheel off the springboard onto the horse followed by a backwards tucked somersault in the flight-off. The Tsukahara requires an exceptionally speedy run-up and a low flight-on to help your body rotate effectively.

TSUKAHARA PIKED
The piked Tsukahara is performed with the flight-off in the piked position. Body rotation with the pike is slightly slower than with the tuck as the body presents a larger area in flight. You will need a great deal of experience to perform both versions.

Nadia Comaneci performs her own version of the Radochla somersault on the asymmetric bars—from high bar to high bar.

Asymmetric bars

Until the 1930s, women gymnasts used to exercise on the parallel bars which were designed in the 19th century with men in mind.

Then before the last war, the heights of the two bars were changed so that they would be more suited to the strength limitations of women.

The new bars were shown at the 1936 Olympic Games in Berlin and were first used in the Olympics of 1952.

Since then, exercises on the asymmetric bars have developed on spectacular lines, more like those of the men's high bar than those of the parallel bars. The greatest performer of modern times on the asymmetrics is Nadia Comaneci of Romania who achieved perfect scores at the 1976 Montreal Olympics.

The asymmetric bars is the hardest piece of apparatus for women gymnasts to master. To perform the advanced moves, you need considerable courage and, more than for the other three pieces, strong arms and shoulders.

This is because you have to swing your body in a variety of movements smoothly and quickly from bar to bar. And training for the bars, if you do not take care, can produce callouses on your hands and bruises on your thighs and hips.

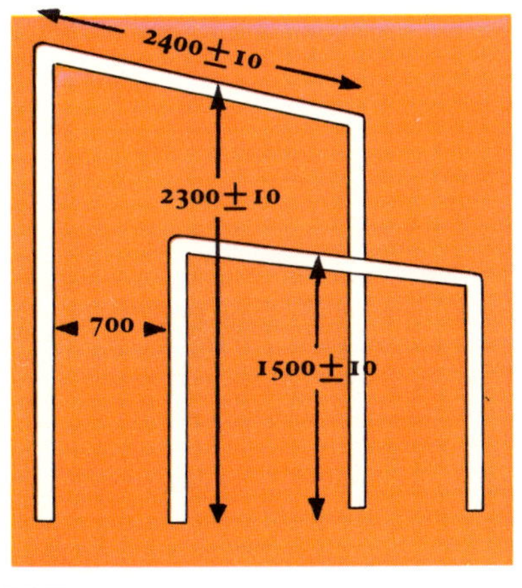

Training

Your training for the asymmetric bars should include an exercise to make you stronger in the arms and shoulders. Here are two ideas.

Press-ups In the front support position on the floor, lower and raise your body with your arms six times.

Pull-ups Holding on to a high bar with your feet clear of the floor, pull your body up to touch the bar with your chin. Lower and repeat six times.

You will also need to be able to bend easily from the hips. The exercise shown on p. 11 for your legs is a good one for this purpose.

Get to know the positions shown on this page. They will be useful to you later when you are learning advanced moves and competition routines.

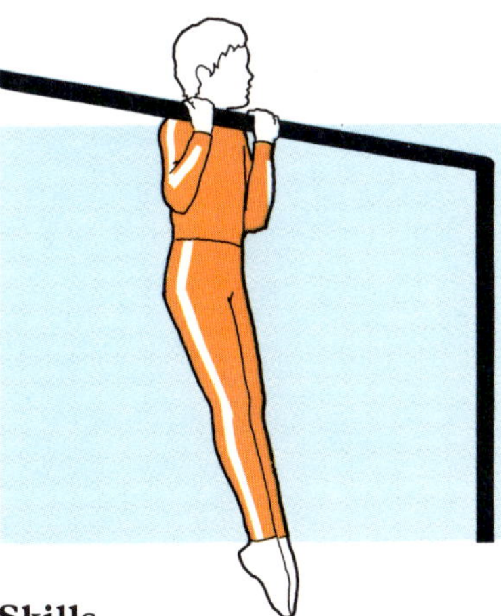

Skills

The next stage is to learn some basic skills on one bar. First, get used to swinging backwards and forwards. Change your grips, at the end of a swing, one hand at a

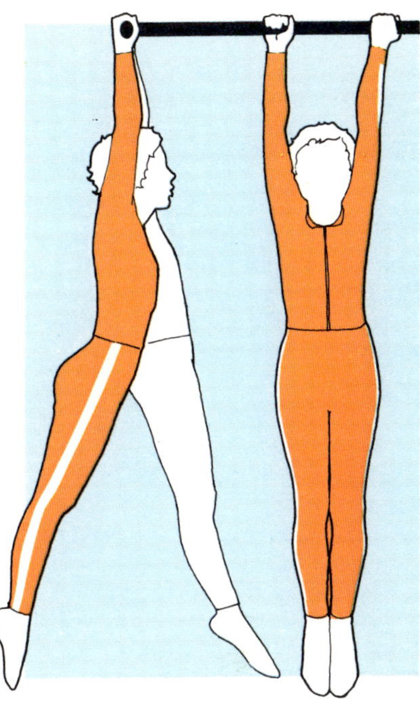

time, so that your body is making half-turns. Then try circling the bar from the front support and mill support positions. Next, practise circling and swinging up

to the front support position from the ground. With your coach, you should also learn to straddle, squat and handstand on the bar.

LONG UNDERSWING AND UPSTART
This mount allows you to swing forward and back to front support. With your hands in a regular grip, jump back into a piked position. Swing forward, stretching out your legs and then pike again quickly, bringing your toes up to the bar. Swing your legs downward, taking your body up and onto the bar ready for the next move.

STRADDLE JUMP TO LONG HANG
Take off from the springboard to place your hands on the low bar. As in the straddle vault, push off the low bar as you straddle over. Quickly reach for the high bar and swing into the long hang. Or, once you have grasped the high bar, perform an upstart.

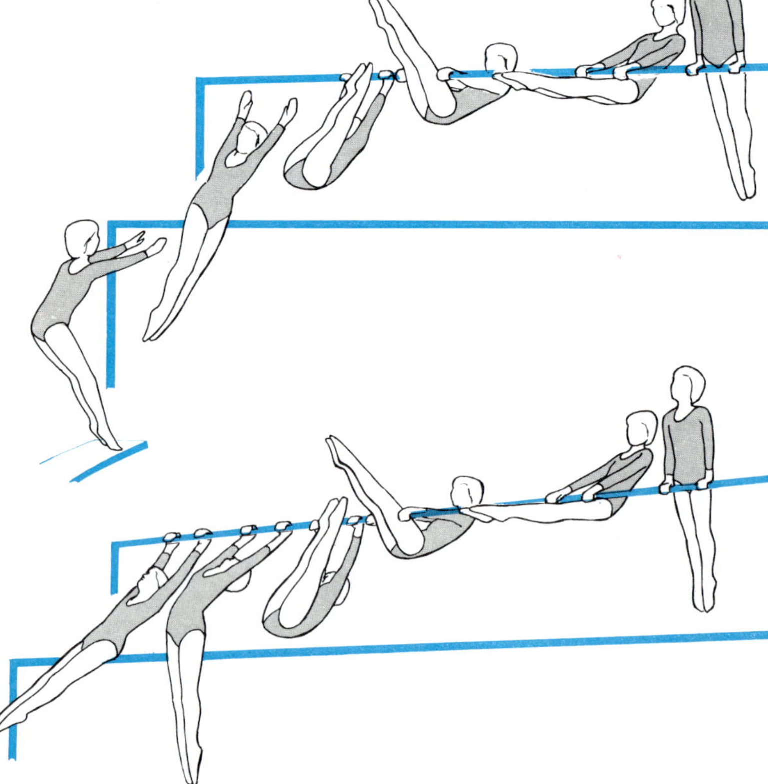

FREE JUMP TO FRONT SUPPORT ON HIGH BAR
With a run-up, jump from the springboard clear of the low bar, executing a half turn and reaching for the high bar. As you grasp the high bar in regular grip, pike your body, bringing your toes up to the bar. Let your legs fall forward, and then swing up to front support.

UPSTART FROM LOW BAR TO HIGH BAR
From the back lying position, hands in regular grip, push your legs back and then forward speedily into a piked position, swinging backwards from the low bar. Then bring your legs down and swing into front support on the high bar, pressing down with your arms.

BACK SEAT CIRCLE
In the back support position on the low bar, and with your hands in regular grip, raise your body to a piked position. Then drop your body backwards to circle the bar, unfolding to the back support position again on completion of the circle.

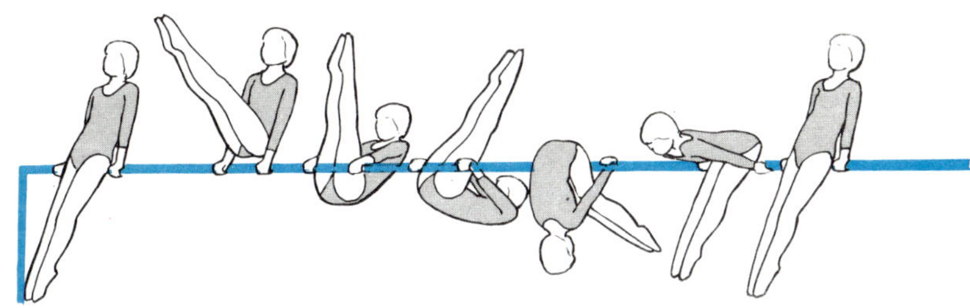

FRONT SEAT CIRCLE
From the back support position, reverse grip, on the low bar, raise your legs to pike over the bar. Fall forward to circle the bar, straightening your legs at the top of the circle to bring your body once more to the back support position.

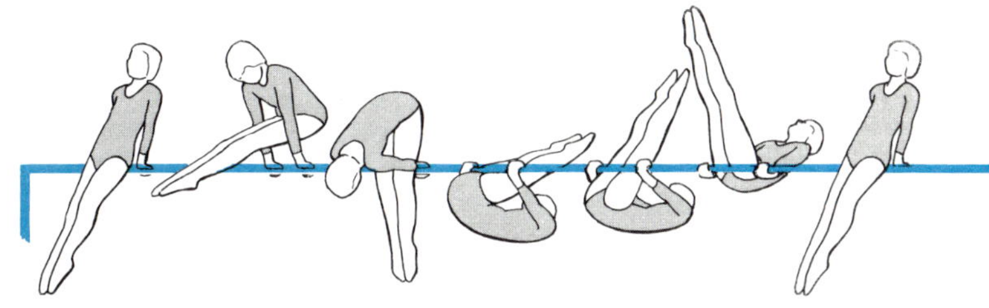

REAR LYING TO BACK SUPPORT ON HIGH BAR
From rear lying, regular grip, pike your body fast and stretch your legs through your arms. As the swing takes your body under the high bar, extend your legs up and over so that your body follows through to back support.

HANDSTAND FROM LOW BAR TO HIGH BAR
Stand on the low bar with your hands on the high bar in regular grip. Push with your legs, piking your body, up to handstand. You can perform a handstand from the high bar to the low bar by swinging forward from front support in a piked position.

LONG SWING AND BACKWARD HIP CIRCLE
To learn this move you *must* have support or mats. From front support on the high bar, swing· your legs forward. As you swing back, push your arms up and away and swing down to a long hand, body straight. On meeting the low bar, pike around it, transferring your grasp from the high bar, to front support.

DISLOCATION CATCH
The dislocation catch follows on from the previous movement and is more spectacular. You pike around the low bar as before, but without holding it, to catch the high bar behind you. Your body must arch for the catch. This movement takes a great deal of practice and confidence to achieve.

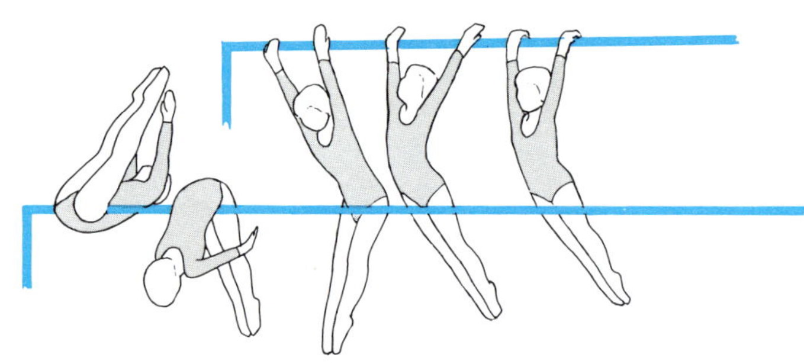

FRONT SUPPORT STRADDLE TO REAR SUPPORT
From front support to the high bar, swing your legs back and up so that they straddle your hands. When your seat is over the bar, bring your hands outside your legs quickly and grip the bar again. Try to regrasp smoothly. Then straighten to rear support.

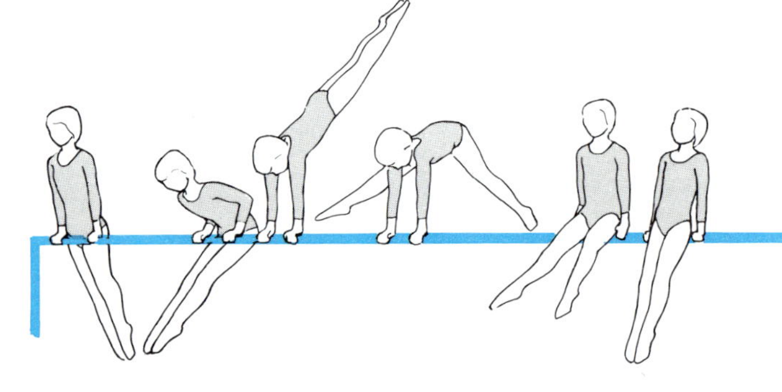

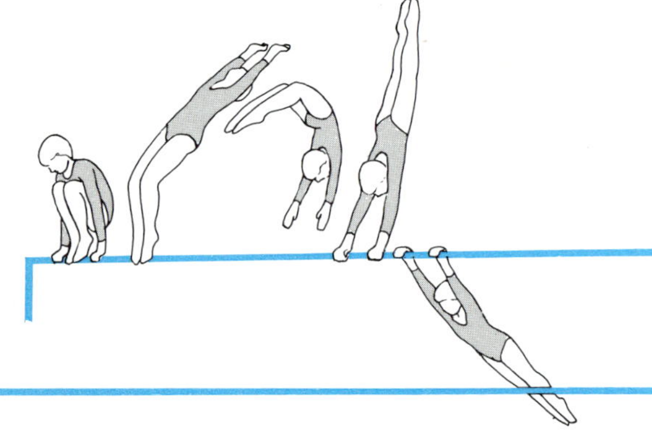

KORBUT SOMERSAULT
This is a movement made famous by the immortal Olga Korbut. You squat on the high bar, somersault back to catch the high bar, and then swing down to long hang.

RADOCHLA
Named after the East German gymnast Brigette Radochla, this movement can be a mount or part of a routine. It is basically a forward straddle somersault from the low bar to the high bar. Nadia Comaneci has perfected it as a somersault from high bar to high bar.

UNDERSWING DISMOUNT
Here is a dismount which can be performed from either low or high bar. From front support, shoot your shoulders back, pike your hips and thrust your legs upwards and forwards. When your arms are stretched, let go for the landing. Remember to land the same way as in vaulting.

HANDSTAND DISMOUNT
From front support on the high bar, reach out and grasp the low bar in mixed grip—right hand regular, left hand in reverse. Swing up to a handstand then release the right hand to quarter turn to land sideways.

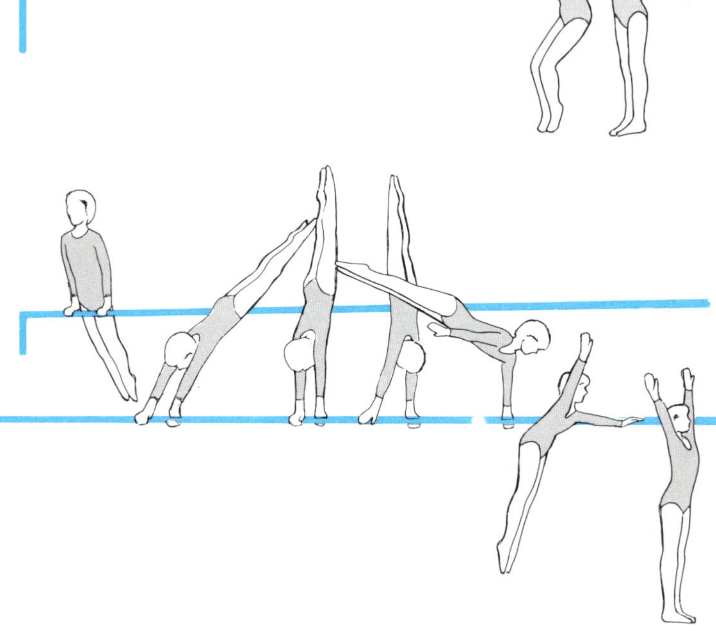

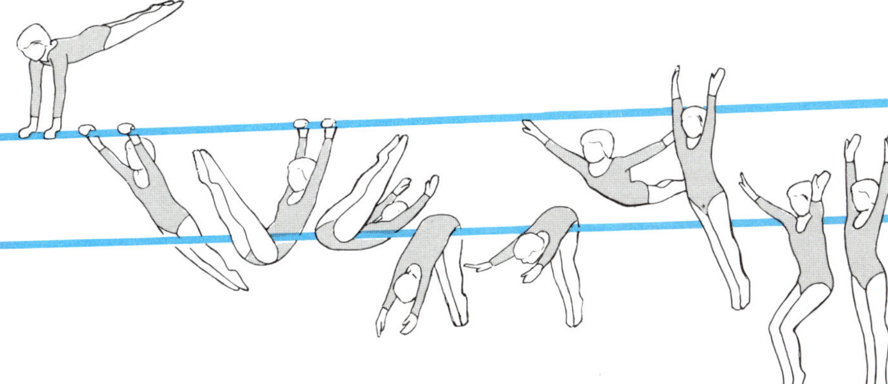

HECHT DISMOUNT
This is a long swing down to pike around the low bar without holding, to arch forward for the landing (see the previous diagram on the dislocation catch). On your rotation off the low bar, remember to lift your legs as well as your arms and body.

Balance beam

The balance beam is the only piece of gymnastic apparatus that was developed exclusively for women. Its main purpose as its name implies, is to test the balancing ability of the gymnast as she performs a sequence of moves on it.

A version of the beam was used by Pehr Ling, the Swedish gymnastics pioneer, in the mid-19th century. This beam aimed to allow women to demonstrate simple balances. The greatest advance, however, has been since World War Two, when leading gymnasts showed that movements performed on the floor can also be performed on the beam.

Today, a beam exercise should contain a fluid 'balance' of movements: jumps, turns, balances and dance steps as well as moves linked with tumbling such as handstands.

All these movements have to be performed on a narrow platform 10cm wide and 5m long, raised 110cm off the ground.

No wonder that even the best gymnasts in the world fall off the beam at times during a competition. A fall from the beam costs a deduction of 0.5 points and the fallen gymnast must remount the beam within ten seconds.

The whole exercise must last between 75 and 95 seconds. It must be continuous, but a total of three pauses are allowed for moves such as handstands.

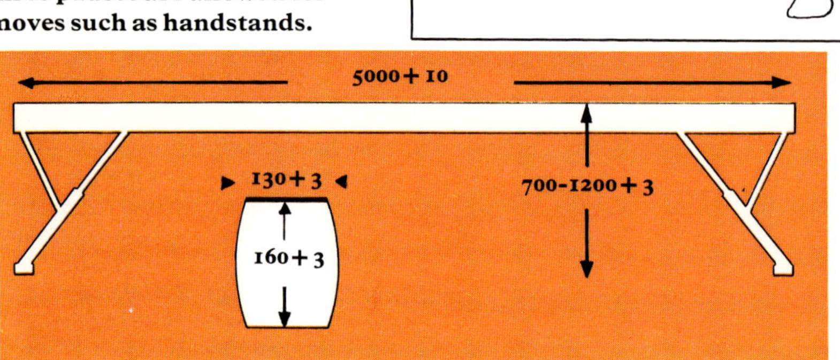

Preparation

When you watch a top gymnast performing on the beam, you will notice that her legs are very supple. It is important that you should have supple legs for beam work, too.

This is because many balances require your legs to bend straight from the hips. So aim to perfect your splits—right, left and side splits—as part of your training for the beam. But do so only when your body is warmed up.

Exercises

These exercises will help you supple and strengthen your legs.

1 Put the heel of one leg on a raised edge such as a bar or beam and slide your foot along. This will stretch the muscles of the leg. Now repeat with the other leg.

2 When in the splits position, put your front leg on a raised object such as a rolled mat. Lean over your front leg. Then place your back leg on the mat and lean backwards.

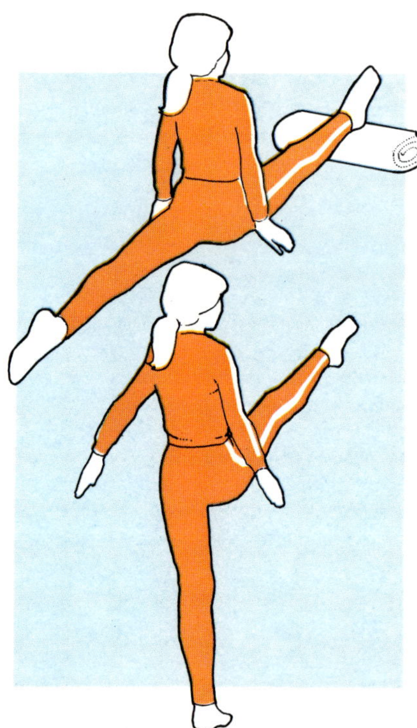

3 Point one leg forward, then lift and hold it as high as possible, keeping both legs straight and your back upright. You must not hold onto anything for support. Repeat, using both legs, to the back and side.

Training

When you first start training for the beam, remember that many of the movements are best learned on the floor.

If you have learned some floor exercise skills, try them on a line drawn on the floor or on a bench, or on a low beam if there is one available.

Then you can try the skills on a full-size beam. Remember to move at a fairly slow pace and to keep your head up.

Get used to working on the beam, even if you just walk up and down it at first. And be prepared to fall off—often.

FRONT SUPPORT MOUNT
Facing the beam, jump up to front support with your hands in line with your shoulders. Swing your right leg over the beam, changing your grip, to straddle sit. From here, you can progress on to other movements, for example a V sit. The front support mount is one of the simplest to learn.

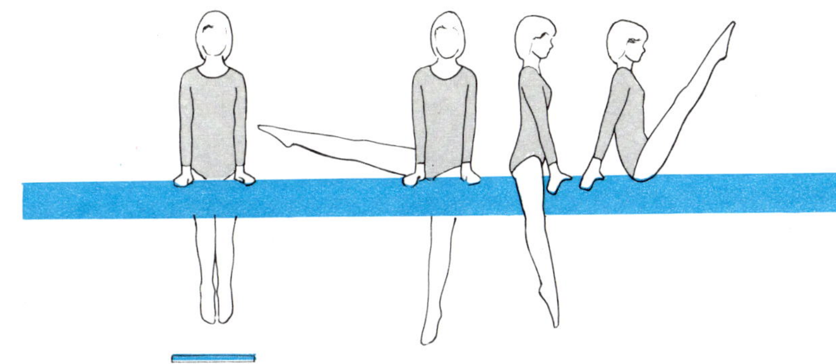

FORWARD ROLL VAULT MOUNT
Take off with both feet from a springboard on to the end of the beam. Place your hands on the beam with the thumbs on top. Tuck your head under as you start the roll. As you come out of the roll, put your right foot on the beam and come up to a standing position.

CARTWHEEL
You should first learn the cartwheel along a line on the floor before you take it on the beam. The hands follow each other and must be lifted from the beam as soon as your leading foot takes the weight of your body. While on your hands, you can quarter turn to a handstand facing along the beam.

BACK WALKOVER
Stand with your arms above you and a foot in front for balance. Drop your head and hands back, while raising your front leg, to grip the beam behind you. Let your legs follow through in the splits position so that your leading foot reaches the beam first. Again, you should first learn this move on the floor.

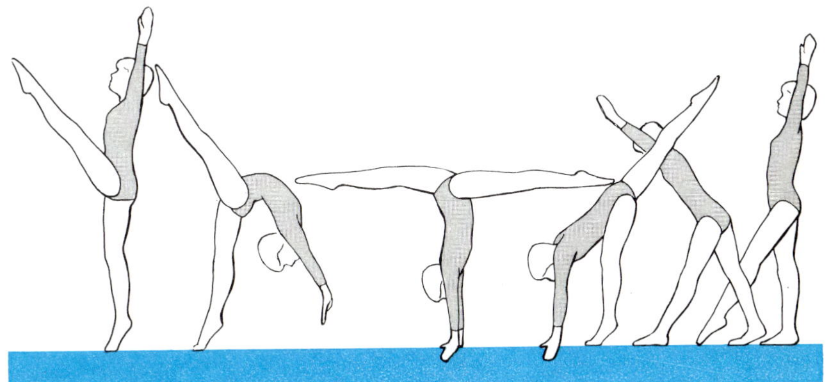

Balance beam

BALANCES

Y

Arabesque

Handstand

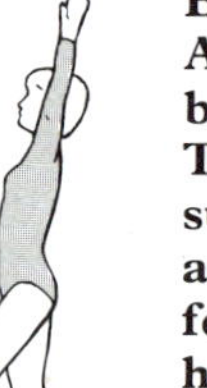

BACK FLIP

As with the cartwheel, learn the back flip along a line on the floor. Then progress to a floor beam surrounded by mats. Swing your arms upwards, push with the feet, and move through a handstand, leading down with one foot to stand upright on both feet.

FRONT SOMERSAULT DISMOUNT

This move needs a run and take-off from both feet. Drive your legs upwards and tuck to help your body rotate. With practice, you can carry out this dismount from other parts of the beam.

BARANI DISMOUNT

If you can perform an aerial cartwheel on the floor, you should have no difficulty in learning this movement from the beam. Push off with your lead foot, throwing the other up. Do not drop your head too much while you rotate. Twist your body on take-off so that you land facing the beam.

Natalia Shaposhnikova of the Soviet Union rivets a Wembley crowd with a one-handed splits handstand on the beam.

Floorwork

During the 19th century, it was fashionable at gymnastics events to stage floor exercises with hundreds or even thousands of performers. These displays were usually held outdoors. When the Modern Olympic Games were introduced in 1896, the same pattern of floor exercises was followed.

However, for reasons of expense, the number of performers was cut down and by 1932, at the Olympic Games in Los Angeles, men gymnasts performed an individual floor exercise for the first time. For women, the individual floor exercise was included at the World Championships in 1950.

The floor exercise is the only event in which men and women use the same apparatus. This is a 12 metre square area which is usually carpeted or specially sprung. The men's exercise lasts from 50 to 70 seconds while the women's routine, which is performed to music, lasts from 60 to 90 seconds.

For both men and women, the floor exercise must be a blend of movements performed over the whole area. Women must combine leaps, turns and tumbling skills with dance movements, while men must include strength and balance elements with their tumbling.

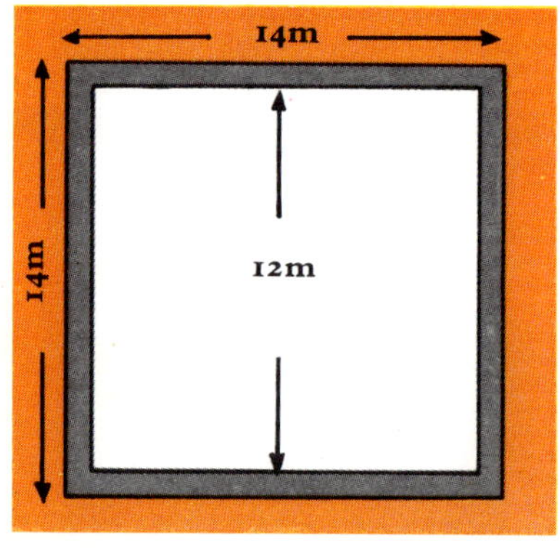

Training

For men, the floor exercise opens a gymnastics competition. For women, it is the finale. For both, the floor exercise contains movements which are the heart of gymnastics and which are the base of routines on other apparatus.

That is why young gymnasts always start by learning the elements of the floor exercise. That is also why exercises more related to the floor, such as the warm-up exercises on page 11, will help you become supple and strong and a good all-round gymnast.

As you will know, one of the qualities you need to be a good gymnast is stamina. In the floor exercise, you have to perform many movements without becoming tired. So set yourself the goal of practice, practice and more practice of your floor skills. This will help you build up your physical endurance.

For young gymnasts, training should include learning basic positions and flexibility. On this page are examples of basic positions which, once learned, can lead onto the next stage: developing movements and then sequences for the full floor exercise.

On the following pages are examples of movements, many of which, particularly the tumbling ones, can be performed by both boys and girls.

Basic positions
Starting and finishing:
1 Arms extended
2 Front prone
3 Back prone
4 Front support
5 Back support
6 Straddle stand
7 Shoulder stand
8 Headstand
9 Long sit
10 Upright sit
Basic flexibility
11 Lumbar fold
12 Japana
13 Bridge
14 Left splits
15 Right splits
16 Side splits
17 Shoulder stretch

Music and dance
Leading clubs give their girl gymnasts some ballet training because dance movements are such an important element of the women's floor exercise.

So, too, is the music which girls and their coaches select for their routine.

The music—which must be played on one instrument (the electric piano, accordian and organ are not allowed)—must be varied in speed and rhythm and fit the personality of the gymnast.

For example, catchy, pop-type music would suit a small, lively kind of girl better than serious ballet music.

So be on the look-out for music that you like and could use for your floor routine. It could make a winning difference to you in a competition.

Composition
In a major competition, floor exercises have to be composed according to the rules laid down by the Code of Points.

For both boys and girls, it is a good idea to include some original ways of linking the moves of your routine.

You should also make the most of moves which you can perform really well. But remember that you must try to perfect any weak points you have in moves or positions.

Elena Naimushina is a gifted young Soviet gymnast who makes the most of her elfin looks during her floor exercise.

FORWARD ROLL
With arms and fingers pointing forwards, crouch down and place your hands on the floor. Tuck your head between your arms and take your weight on your hands. Push with your feet so that you roll forwards on your shoulders. Raise your feet as high as you can, tuck your body and roll to stand without using your arms.

BACKWARD ROLL
Crouch down in a tucked position, body weight and arms forward. Roll backwards, keeping your back rounded and place your arms by your head, fingers pointing towards the shoulders. Push strongly with your hands to help raise your hips. Practise rolling on to your knees first, and then to your feet.

HANDSTAND
Lift your arms straight above your head and take a long step forwards. Kick your back leg up and when your hands are on the floor—shoulder width apart—push up with your leading leg. Aim to make a straight line with your legs, body and arms so do not raise your head or let your arms bend.

BACKWARD ROLL TO HANDSTAND
From the standing position, bend your knees and roll backwards, quickly placing your arms by your head. As your shoulders touch the mat, push upwards with your legs held straight. The momentum should carry you to the handstand. Some gymnasts can perform this movement with straight arms.

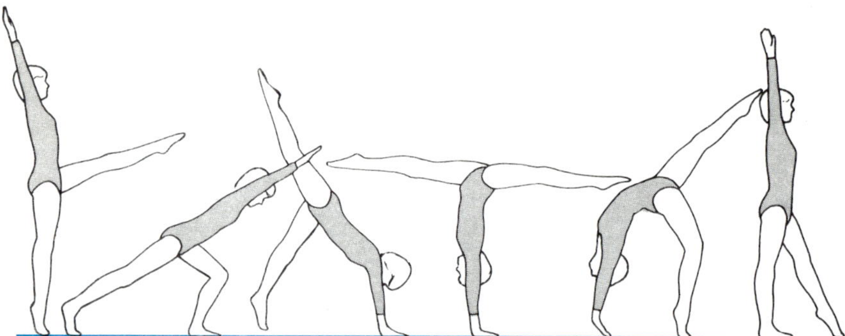

WALKOVER
This move starts with a handstand. However, keep your leading leg moving over your head so that both legs are in the splits position. Let your leading leg come down to the floor and push with your hands so that your body comes upright. Keep your second leg high as you straighten up.

CARTWHEEL
The cartwheel is a combination of handstand and walkover except that it is a sideways movement. Imagine yourself as a wheel moving along a straight line with your arms and legs as spokes. Your arms and legs must follow each other as evenly as possible. Your hips must be held high when your legs move.

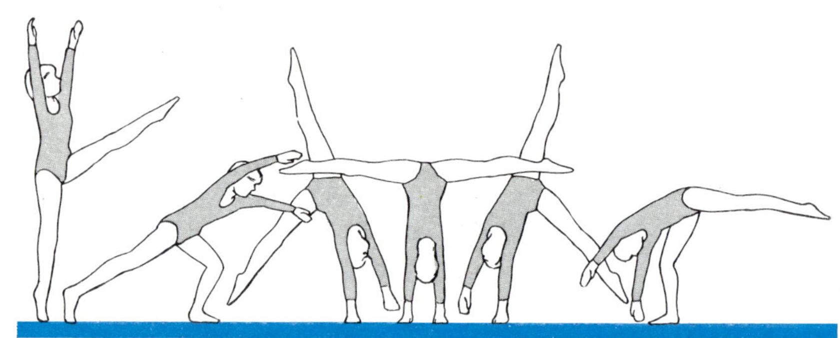

ROUND-OFF
The round-off is a fast cartwheel except when your body is upside down, your legs are brought together and you make a quarter turn inwards. This means that when your legs come down and you are upright again, you face the direction of the start of your run. Remember to push firmly from your hands.

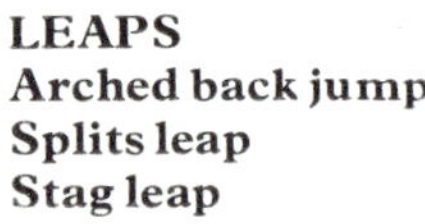

LEAPS
Arched back jump
Splits leap
Stag leap

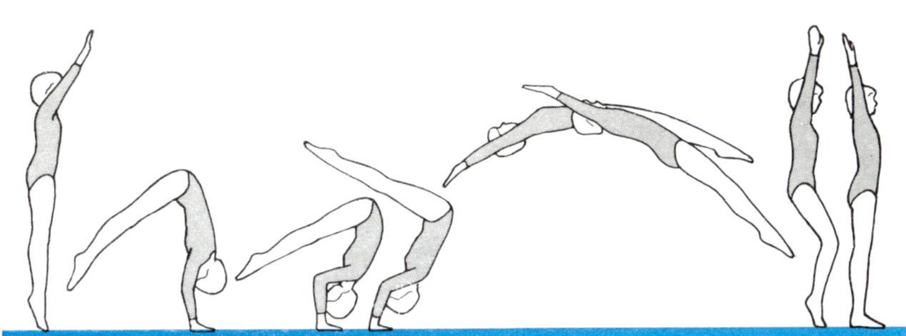

HEADSPRING

Start in a tucked position. Put your head between your hands and bring your legs up quickly while at the same time pushing forcefully with your hands. The action will bring you back to the tucked position, provided you let your hips fall forwards. Later, practise the headspring from the standing position.

FRONT HANDSPRING

Once you have mastered the handstand confidently, you can learn the handspring which is a faster version. When your legs reach the handstand position, they must be together. Push hard with your hands so that your body lifts up and over and you land on the balls of your feet in the upright position.

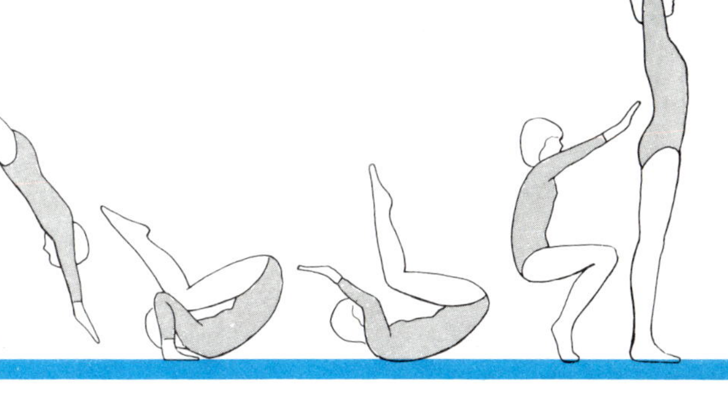

DIVE FORWARD ROLL

This movement can be performed from a standing position or from a run. Achieve enough height so that you can tuck your head under your body as you begin the roll. The momentum of the roll will bring you back to a standing position. Try and imagine that you are diving over an obstacle.

BACK FLIP

From the standing position, bend your knees and lean back. Swing your arms upwards while forcing your body into the air with your hips forward. Stretch with your arms and bring your body through the handstand position. Push with your hands off the floor and bring your legs down together to stand.

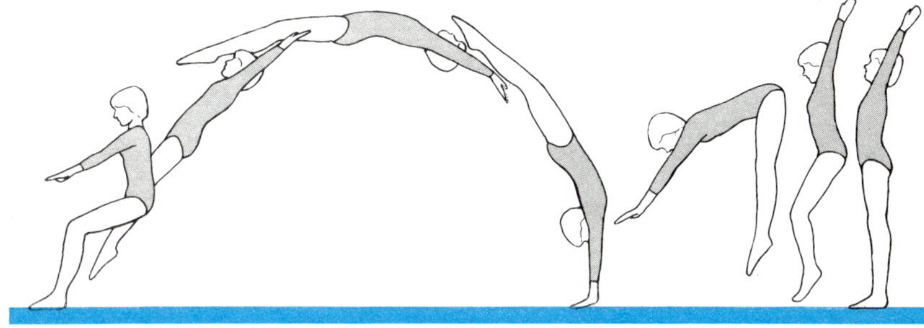

BACK WALKOVER

Lift your arms above your head and raise one leg high in front of you. Bend back to place your hands on the floor. Follow through with your second leg so that both legs are in the splits position. Push with your hands, bringing your leading leg to the floor and your body upright, second leg horizontal.

FRONT SOMERSAULT

At first, practise this movement on a crash mat with a springboard or trampette. Obtain plenty of height with your leap and reach forward with your arms. At the top of your leap, grasp your knees and rotate in a tucked position. As your head comes up, straighten your legs and arms for the landing.

BACKWARD SOMERSAULT

In the standing position, lower your arms and bend your legs. Then jump up, swinging your arms above you and throwing your head back. Tuck your knees into your chest, grasping them with your arms. Rotate in this tucked position and when the turn is almost complete, straighten your body to land.

AERIAL CARTWHEEL

To perform this fast variety of cartwheel, you will need speed together with a strong push-off from the floor with your leading leg. Your back leg must rise quickly to be followed around by your leading leg. Practise this movement from a springboard; it is another which needs height for success.

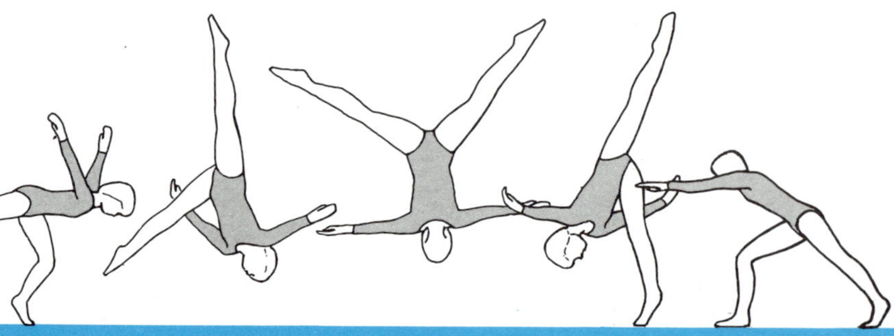

A competent Y balance is the aim of both boy and girl top gymnasts. Girls can perform this balance on beam.

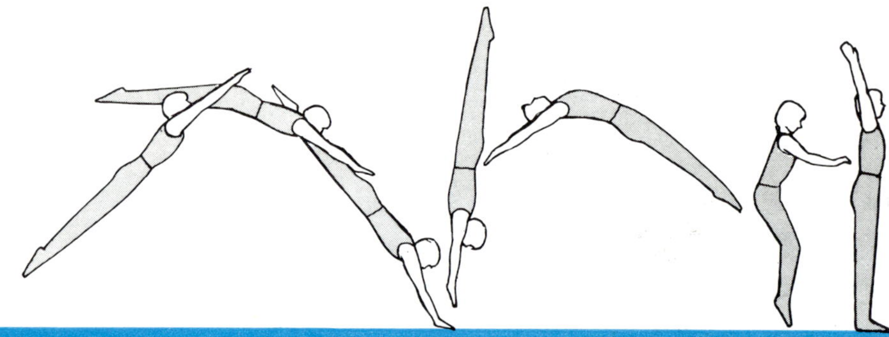

DIVE HANDSPRING
With a run, leap high with your arms above your head into the handstand position. Push hard with your hands when your body weight has moved off the vertical. As you rotate to the standing position, bend your knees for the landing, but then extend your body with arms out and feet together.

JUMP FORWARD TO HANDSTAND
Care must be taken not to over-rotate so that you fall forward. Your arms must take the weight of your body and hold it while your legs come up together to the handstand position. Once you have paused in the handstand, you can proceed to another move. For example, you can complete a forward roll.

ROLL BACKWARD TO HANDSTAND AND SQUAT TO 'L' SUPPORT
This strength move requires you to roll backwards to handstand and then bring your legs down through your arms without touching the floor to 'L' support. You can, of course, reverse this move and move from 'L' support to handstand as shown on the next page.

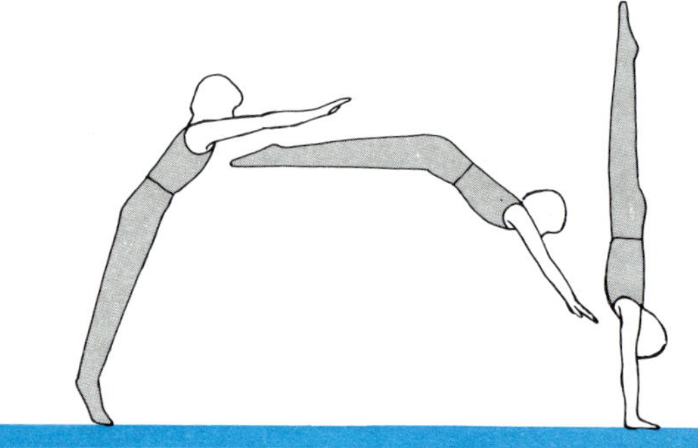

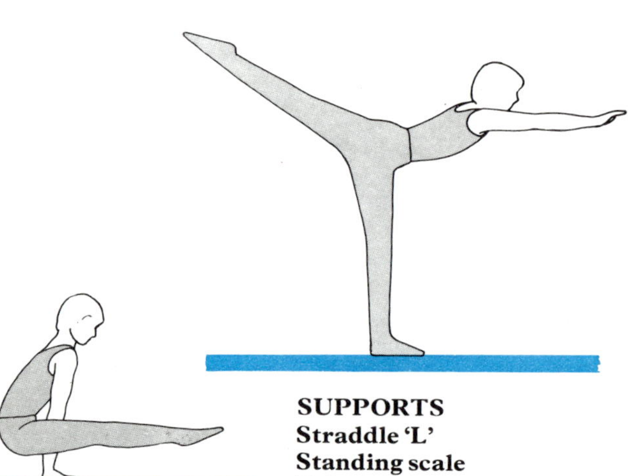

SUPPORTS
Straddle 'L'
Standing scale
Pointed angle sitting

'L' SUPPORT TO HANDSTAND

From 'L' support, squat your legs through your hands, bending forwards so that your body weight remains over your hands. Still bending to counter-balance your weight, raise your legs and extend them, finally straightening out into the handstand position.

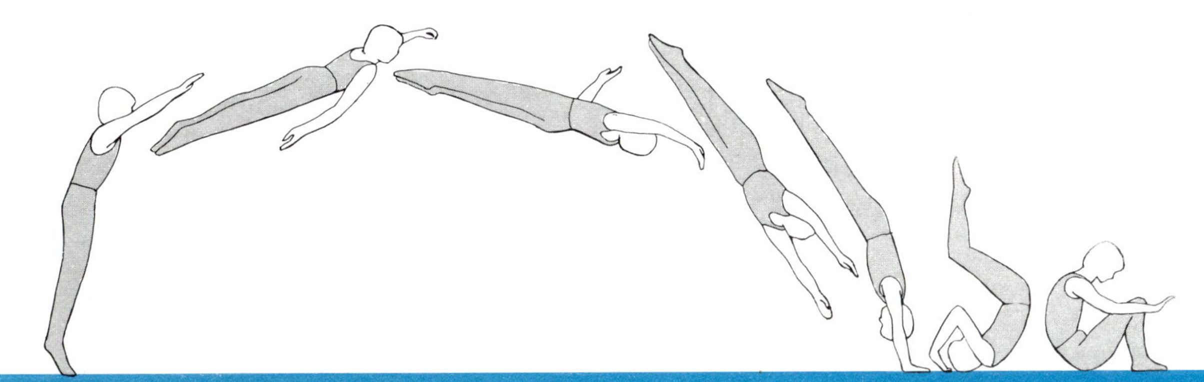

HECHT LEAP FORWARD WITH FULL TURN TO DIVE FORWARD ROLL

You will need a fast run and a powerful take-off for this Hecht leap. As with other similar difficult movements, you will find a springboard most useful to practise this one with. It will also help you to learn the dive forward roll before you try the full turn.

FORWARD TUCKED SOMERSAULT FOLLOWED BY HANDSPRING FORWARD

Here are two movements which are linked together. Obviously you will have to be able to perform each one before you join them. The somersault must pass into the handspring almost as one movement. Remember the limits of the floor area for this one!

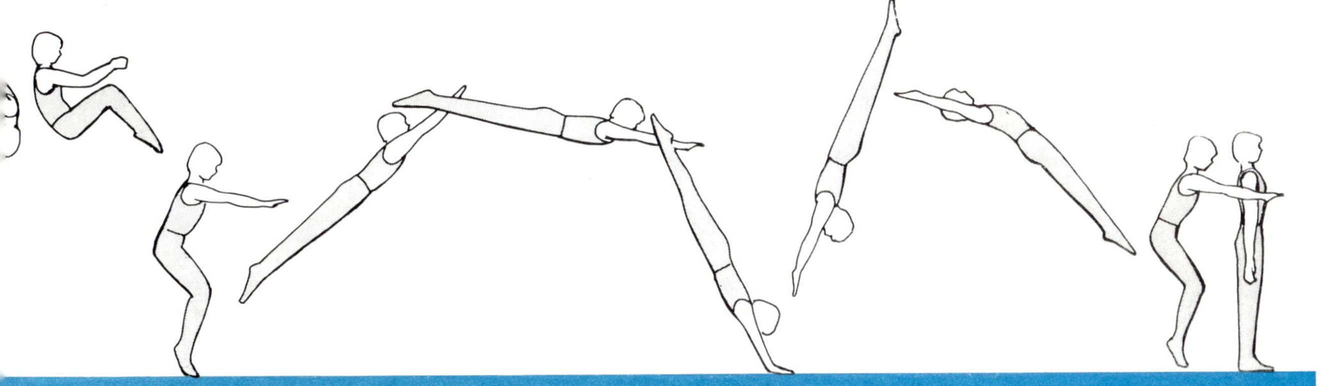

Pommelled horse

The pommelled horse is a piece of men's gymnastic apparatus on which many top gymnasts achieve low scores.

You have to combine strength with balance to perform swinging movements of your legs without stopping. You must also carry out your pommels exercise at a constant speed.

It is no surprise that the pommels take a long time to master and that it is an unpopular piece with many young gymnasts.

Once you can work the pommels, however, you will enjoy the thrill of sweeping round and round and from one end to another.

The modern pommelled horse was developed from the apparatus designed by Ludwig Jahn. Before that, the dummy horse in a wooden form was essential over many centuries for learning horsemanship.

Cave drawings of ancient Crete show men vaulting live bulls and using the horns as pommels. Today, gymnasts use the pommels to show their skills in other exciting ways.

Using both ends of the horse as well as the pommel handles, you must perform, according to the *Code of Points*, 'undercuts of one leg, circles of one and both legs, and forward and reverse scissors'.

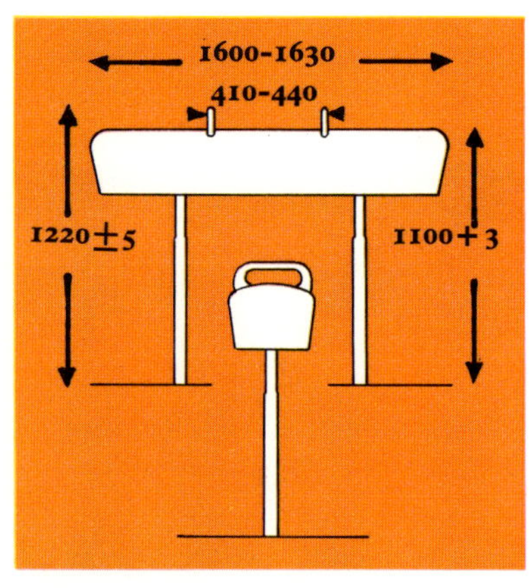

Training

Your training on the pommelled horse must develop your strength and sense of balance at the same time. So start by learning three basic positions.

Front support **1**
Back support **2**
Straddle support **3**

If you find it a strain to hold these positions, your weight—and therefore your balance—is in the wrong place. You can achieve the right balance by moving your shoulders forwards or backwards.

Remember to press down on your hands to stop your shoulders sagging and to keep your legs straight.

The next step is to rock from side to side in these positions. This means pushing and leaving go with one hand as you lean over the opposite side. You will find it easier to start practising in the straddle position.

Keep pushing and rocking until you can do it evenly without falling backwards and forwards and then try in the front and back support positions.

You can also practise rocking on the parallel bars, holding both bars as if they were pommels. Then try moving along the bars, still using this rocking motion.

From the support positions, progress to learning three vaults on the pommelled horse.

Flank vault **4**
Side vault **5**
Front vault **6**

You must master these vaults without a run and to the left and right. Once you can perform them on the pommel handles, attempt these vaults on both ends of the horse.

When you can perform these basic skills with confidence, you can then tackle the moves you will need for competition work.

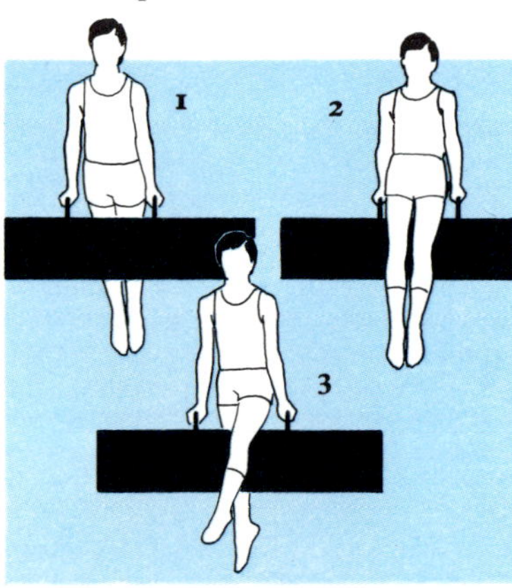

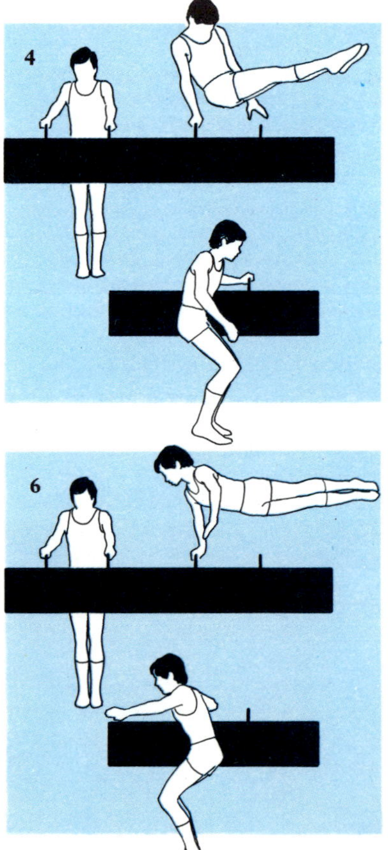

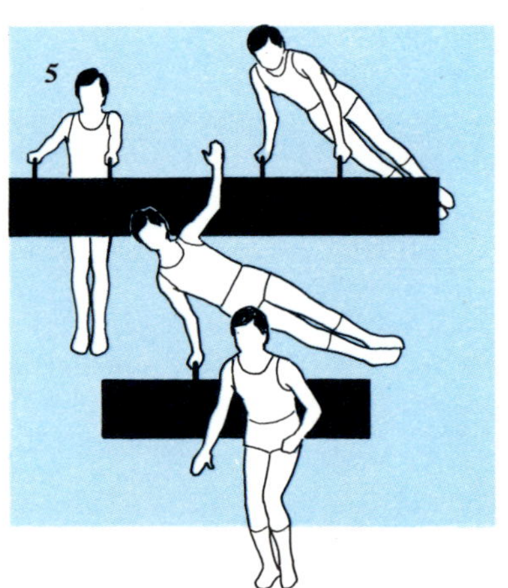

SINGLE LEG CIRCLE
From front support, swing to the right, releasing your left hand. Bring your right leg over the left pommel and regrasp in the straddle position. Lean to the left, and swing your right leg over the right pommel back to front support, releasing and regrasping your right hand.

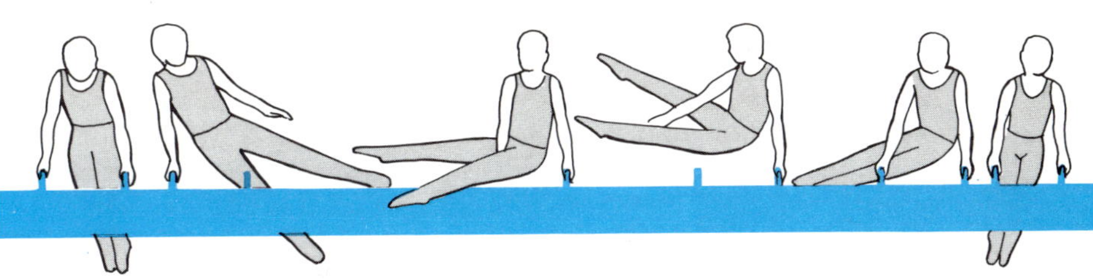

FRONT SHEARS
Swing from front support into the straddle position, right leg over the right pommel. Keep swinging left and switch the position of your legs so that on the swing right, your left leg is in front. Switch your legs again on the right side.

BACK SHEARS
On the reverse shears, your front leg moves against its natural swing. Your right leg would thus swing to the right and your left leg to the left. The back shears is therefore a more difficult movement than the front shears. On both shears swing your legs high before switching back to front.

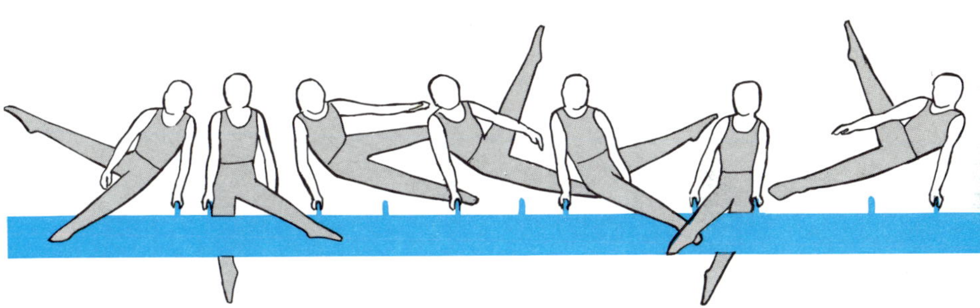

DOUBLE LEG CIRCLE
Keeping your body straight but in a twisting action, swing both legs around the pommelled horse together, letting go with your right or left hand as your legs pass underneath. Your legs must be together. Try single circles first, and then continuous ones. Remember to shift your balance and weight on each swing as you let go and grasp each pommel again. Your head should be held up, too, on this movement. Here are two views of the double leg circle.

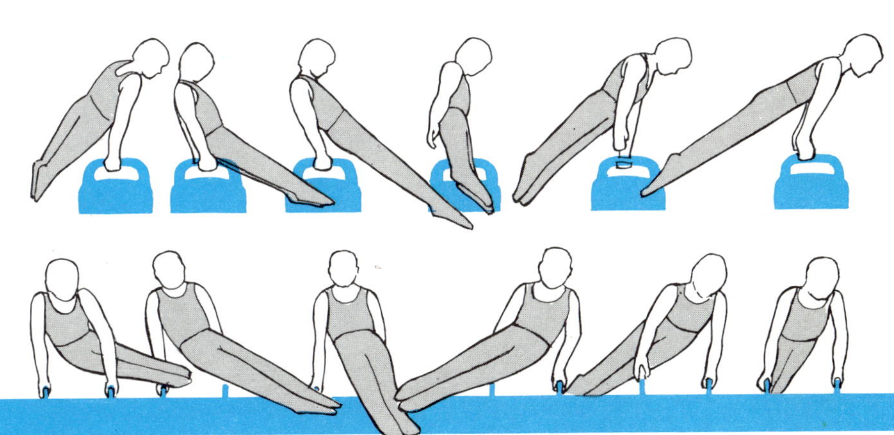

SIDE TRAVEL

The basis of the movement shown here is the double leg circle. As your legs swing around to your left under your left hand, however, regrasp not the left pommel but the right pommel, in front of your right hand. Then transfer your right hand to the right end of the pommel when your legs are behind you.

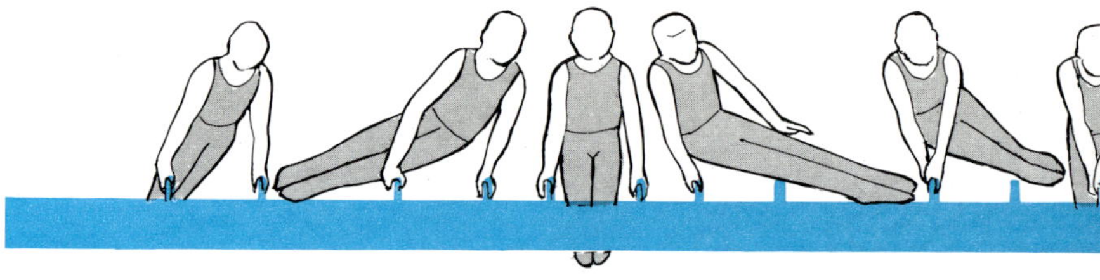

UPWARDS ORIENTED HALF CIRCLE TRAVEL

In this double leg circle, your weight stays on the left side as your body circles the left pommel. Your right hand follows your body, to be placed on the left end of the horse. You are now facing the rear of the horse and can continue circling. Remember to hold your legs high to clear the pommels.

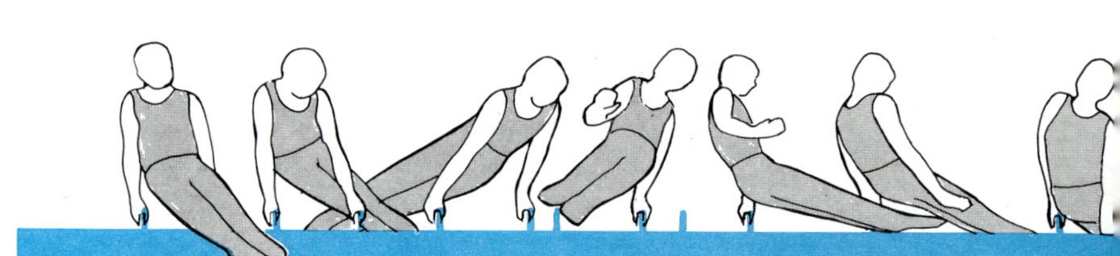

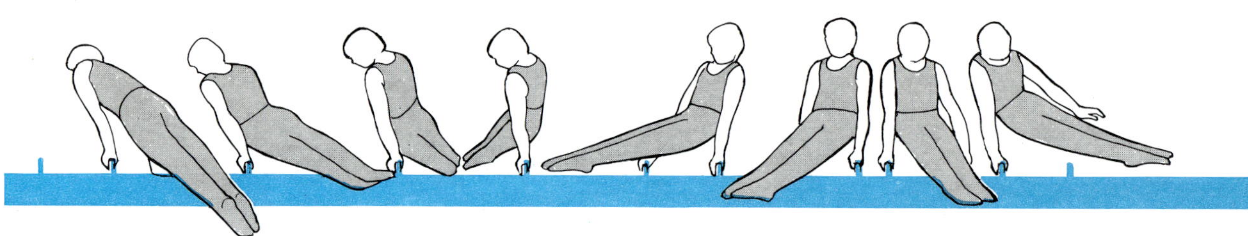

THE STOCKLI

The stockli continues the move above so that you circle the horse once on the end and then swing back to the centre to grasp both pommels again. As your right hand leaves the end of the horse, shift as much body weight as you can to the left to help swing your body up and around easily to the front support position. Your shoulders should lead in these swings.

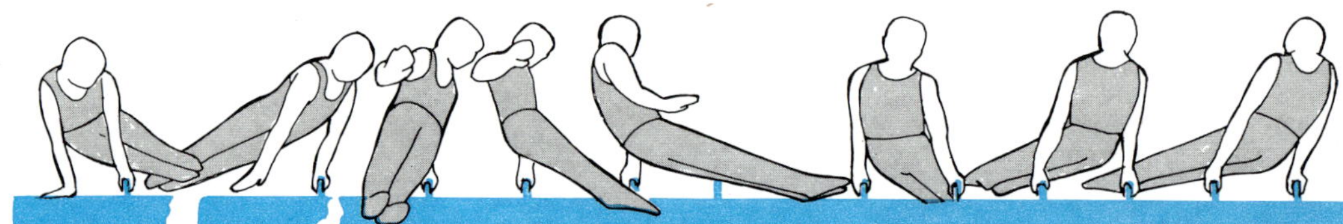

TROMLET

The tromlet combines side travel and upwards oriented half circle travel. You begin with side travel to one end of the horse as before, and then execute a powerful swing to bring you back to rear support on both pommels. The diagram shows you this swing in action.

DISMOUNTS

At the end of your routine, you can use some of the vaults you learned in training as a way to dismount. Shown here are the flank, front and rear vaults.

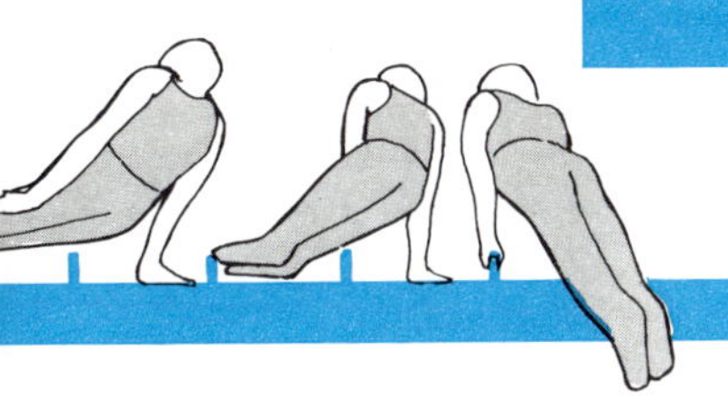

Flank vault
This is a swing up and over the pommels. Remember to shift your balance as your legs move across.

***Front vault* (right)**
In the front vault, extend your free arm to help keep your legs up as you swing around.

***Rear vault* (above)**
Swing your legs over the horse so that you land sideways with one hand holding the rear pommel.

Alexandre Detiatin of the Soviet Union demonstrates side travel on the pommels. This well-known, yet modest international star won the World Cup in 1978 (below).

Rings

Rings require more strength than any other piece of apparatus, but swinging skills have become a major part of a modern rings performance since the Soviet Union introduced them at the Helsinki Olympics in 1952.

Rings came into gymnastics from the circus world as a variation of the trapeze. Jahn included them in his gymnastics programme at the early part of the 19th century.

Today, the rings exercise must contain hold positions as well as swing and strength parts. These must be completed without the gymnast swinging the rings.

Two handstands must be performed, too: one showing strength and the other ending a swing movement. Each has to be held for two seconds.

To be successful on the rings you need to be very strong in your shoulders. This will help you master the strength moves required in competition. It will also help you to keep the rings still as you perform on them. A good sense of timing, too, is an asset on the rings.

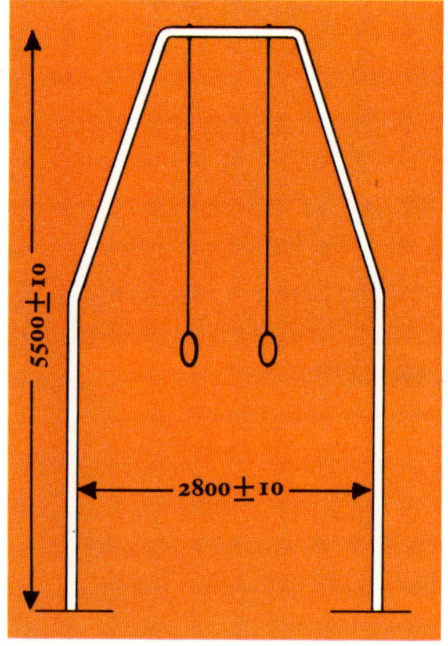

Training

Do not expect to gain all the strength you need for the rings exercise in a short time. You must acquire it gradually by steady practice.

At the same time, you will be practising swinging skills which you will find easier to learn. Young gymnasts are sometimes disappointed that their progress on the rings is not faster. But with regular practice over short periods, there comes a time when the rings cease to be an obstacle to becoming a competent gymnast.

In the early stages of rings training, you should practise on rings which are lowered to head height. As with the other pieces of apparatus, do not attempt difficult moves without a coach or teacher standing by.

Strength positions and moves

Here are some basic positions on the rings which will also help to develop your strength.

Straight hang **1**
Inverted hang **2**
In both these hangs, your body must be straight with toes pointed. For the straight hang, the rings will have to be higher than head height.

Straight arm support **3**
'L' support **4**
Have your coach or teacher help you to jump up to the straight arm support. From here, you lift your legs to the 'L' support position and hold them there for a few seconds.

Once you are used to the straight arm support, move the rings out from your body a little until they—and your arms—shake. Now try and control this shaking. You can also perform this strength move in the 'L' support position.

Chin ups **5**
Skin the cat **6**
Other strength moves to try are chin-ups with legs either straight or in the 'L' position, or skin the cat.

In skin the cat, bring your legs up and between your arms so that they point down behind you. Then bring your legs back to long hang.

Handstand
With the rings adjusted to as low a height as possible, and using a vaulting horse to stand on, practise the handstand on the rings. Someone will have to steady the rings until you become used to holding this key position.

HANG SWING

Your swing moves on the rings must start with a basic skill—swinging on the rings in the hang position. The rings should be high enough so that you clear the floor. Lead with your legs and build up the swing. Open the rings at the top of the swing.

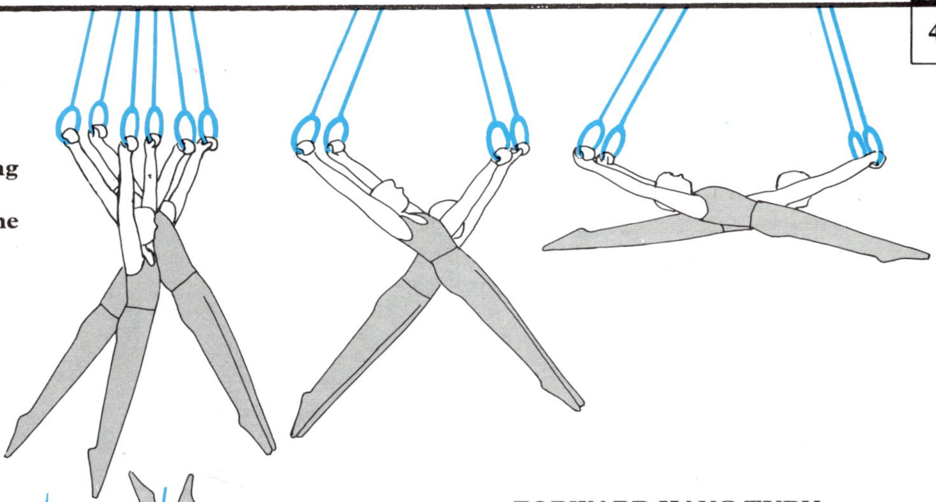

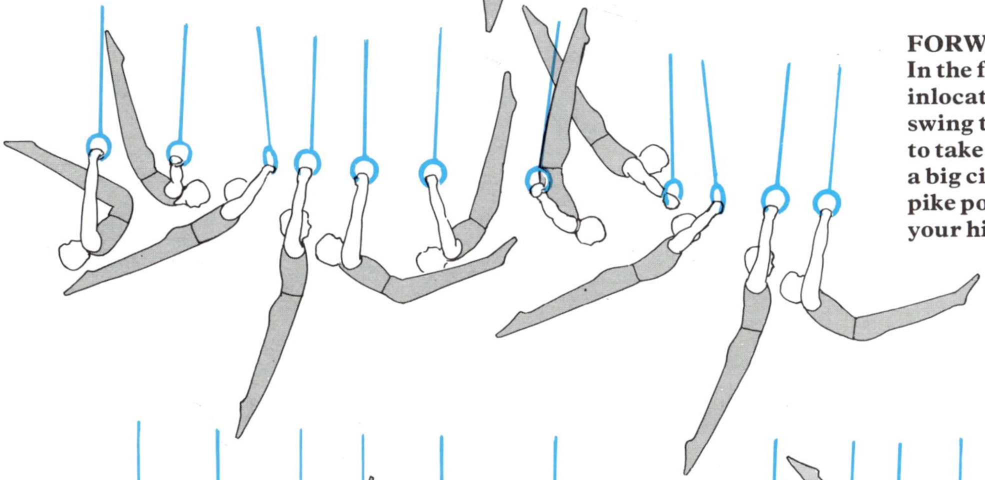

FORWARD HANG TURN

In the forward hang turn or inlocate, you complete a forward swing through the hang position to take your body up and over in a big circle. Start in the inverted pike position and thrust with your hips.

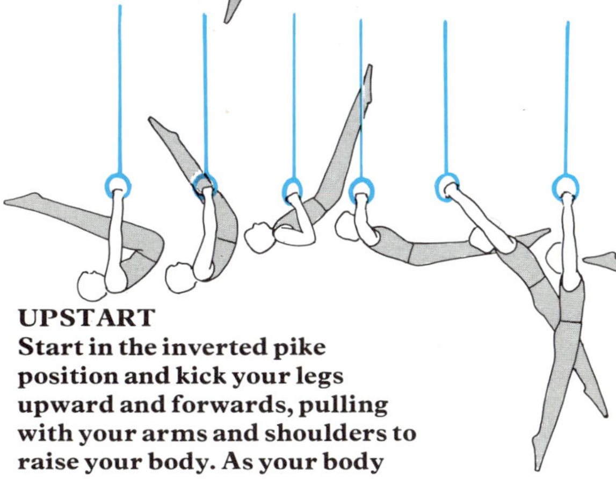

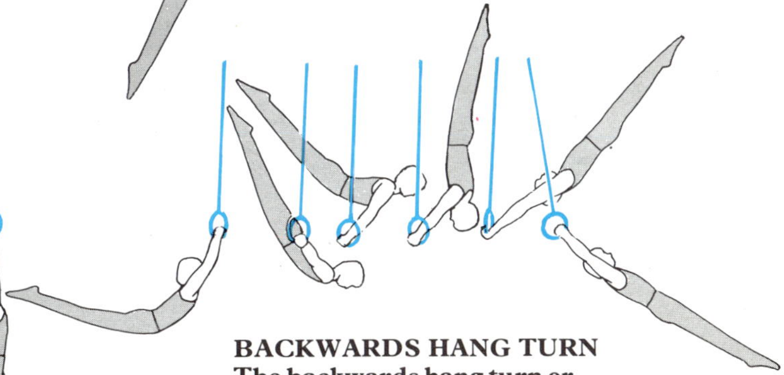

UPSTART

Start in the inverted pike position and kick your legs upward and forwards, pulling with your arms and shoulders to raise your body. As your body swings up, straighten your arms. You can finish in either 'L' or straight arm support.

BACKWARDS HANG TURN

The backwards hang turn or dislocate works in the same way as the forward hang turn except that you swing the other way. Obtain height by lowering your wrists when you extend your arms.

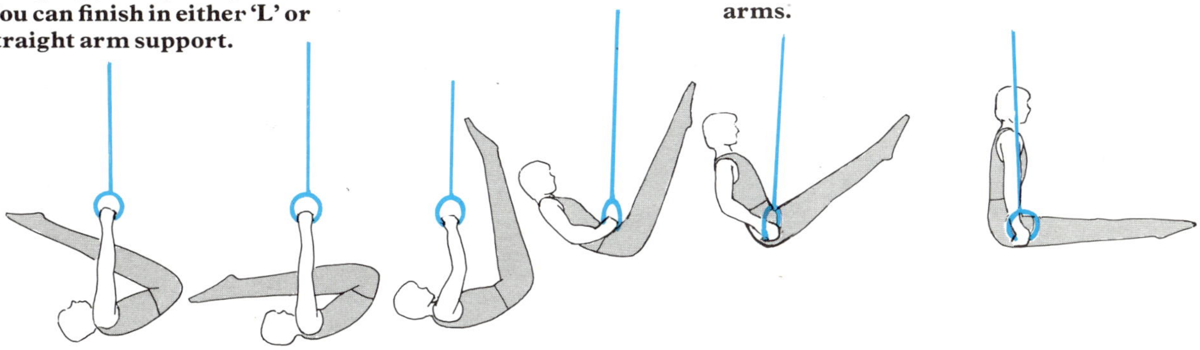

BACK LEVER

In this hold position, your body must be straight and level with the floor. Experts advise that you grip the rings with your palms facing down.

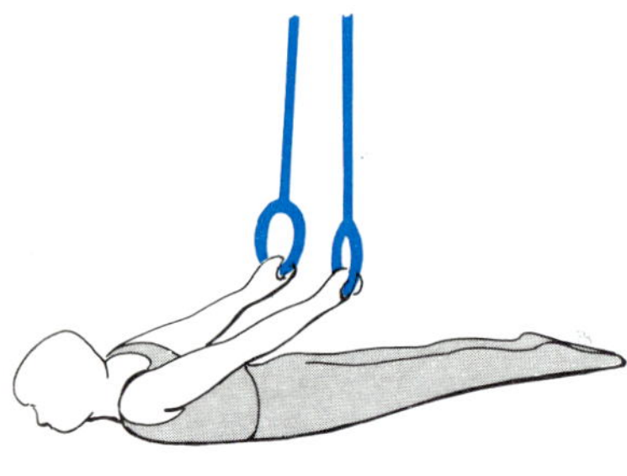

FRONT LEVER

The front lever is harder to hold than the back lever because your joints are more naturally inclined to bend towards the floor in this position.

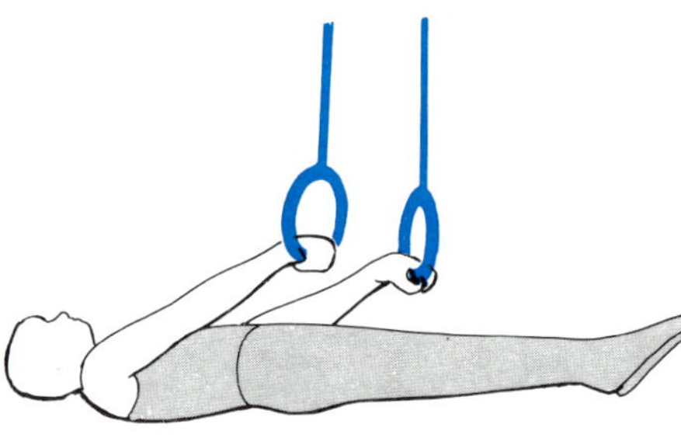

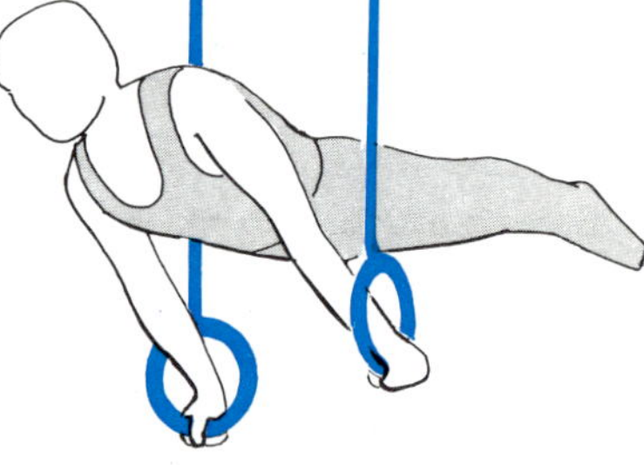

PLANCHE

The planche is another difficult strength hold in which your body has to be held parallel to the floor. You can practise this move on the parallel bars.

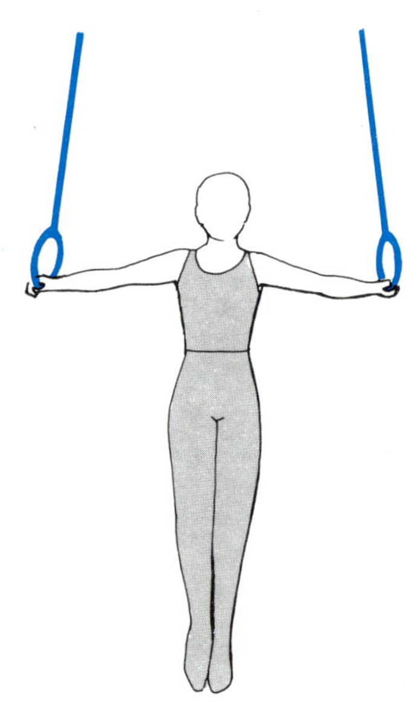

THE CROSS

For many gymnasts, this position is a difficult one to achieve. Your arms must be in a straight line and your body held upright and still for two seconds.

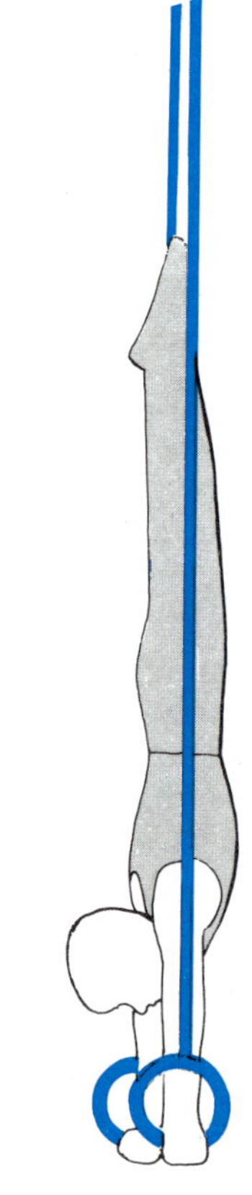

THE HANDSTAND

In performing the handstand on the rings in competition, remember that your hands are the only parts of your body that may touch the apparatus.

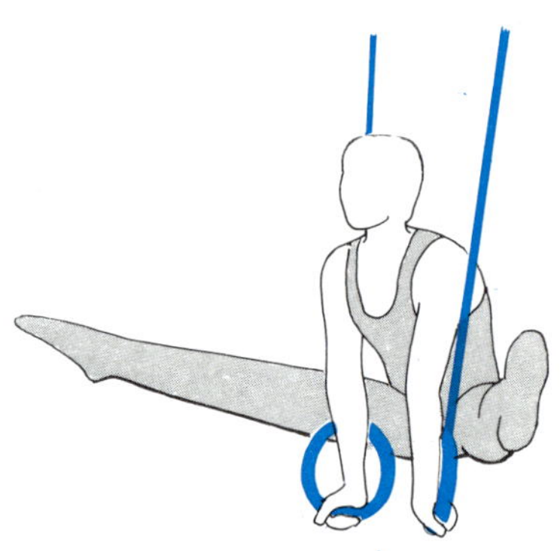

STRADDLE 'L' SUPPORT

This hold differs from the 'L' support position in that you have to keep your balance by leaning your shoulders forward and holding your hips high.

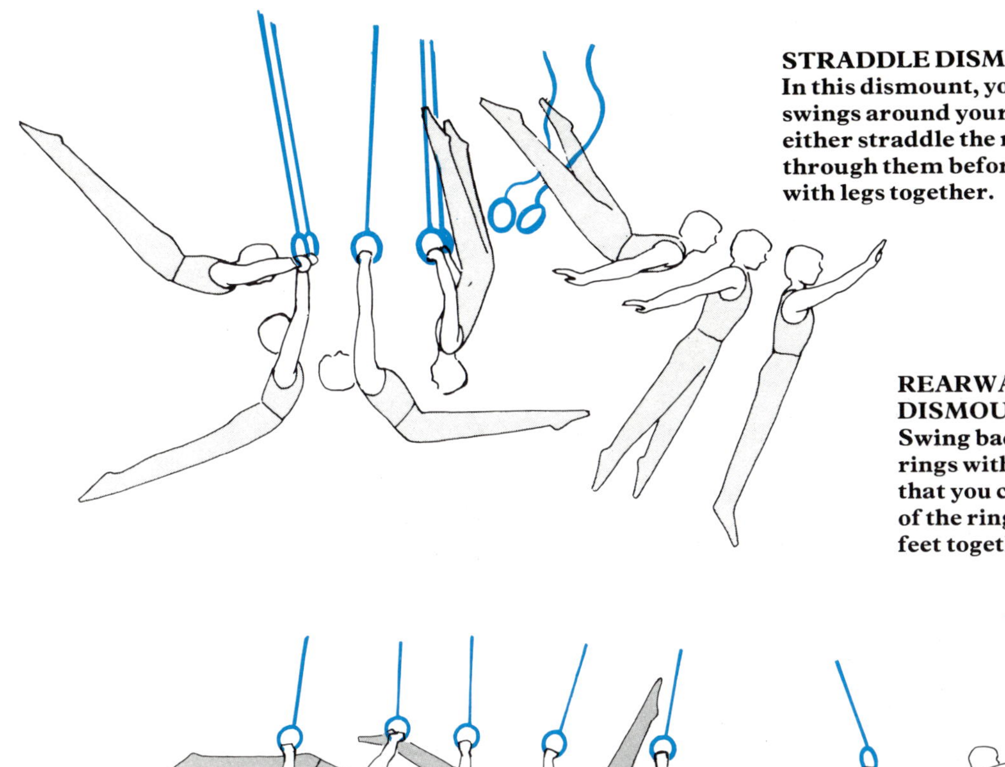

STRADDLE DISMOUNT
In this dismount, your body swings around your hands to either straddle the rings or pass through them before landing with legs together.

REARWARD SWING DISMOUNT
Swing backwards up through the rings with your body extended so that you complete the turn, let go of the rings, and land forward, feet together.

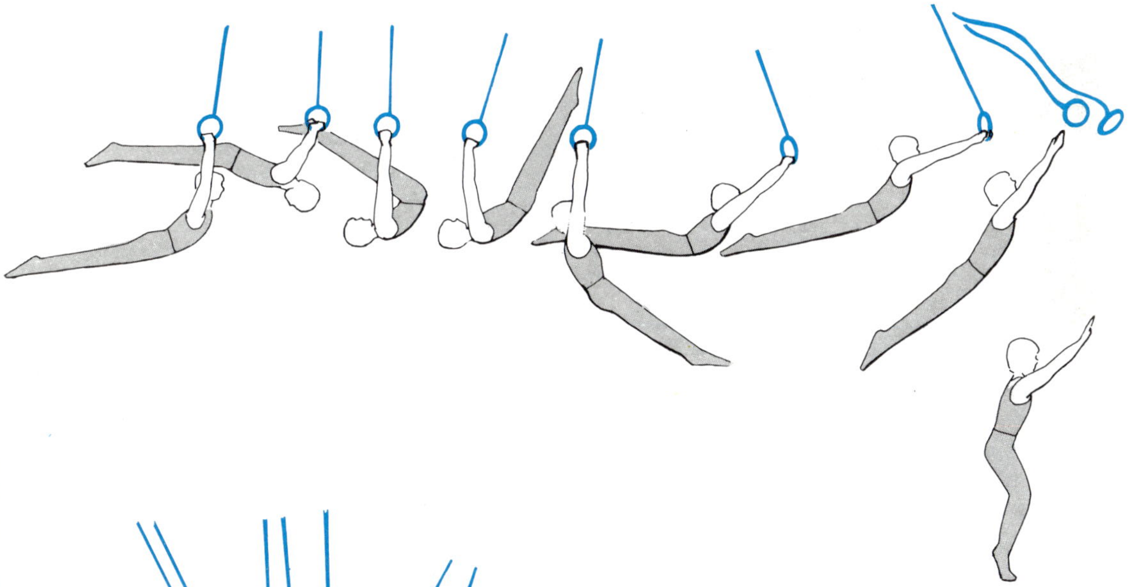

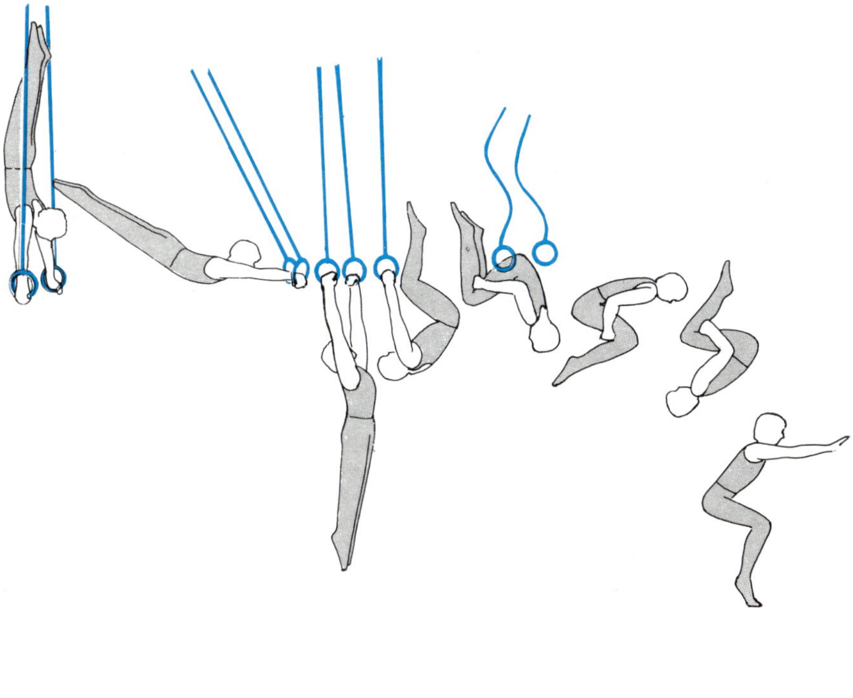

DOUBLE BACK SOMERSAULT DISMOUNT
You need a long swing forward for momentum with a pull on the rings for height. Hold your knees to help rotation, then straighten quickly for landing.

Willy Moy of France shows the planche on rings. This is a difficult strength move which takes much training to achieve.

Parallel bars

The parallel bars were invented almost by chance.

When Ludwig Jahn, the father of gymnastics, developed the pommel horse and its exercises, he found that the young German gymnasts of his day needed more arm and shoulder strength.

So in 1812, Jahn created the parallel bars with the single purpose of preparing gymnasts to perform on the pommels.

Soon the bars became very popular, with women as well as men. During this century, as part of the progress of modern gymnastics, exercises on the parallel bars have changed in style. No longer are strength moves all-important: instead, gymnasts perform a variety of skills.

These skills include movements of support, hang, swing and balance as well as strength. Of these, the swing movements must take up most of the exercise. The gymnast can also perform up to three 'holds' which must be held, as you would expect, for a duration of two seconds.

In fact, the make-up of movements in a parallel bars routine makes this apparatus a favourite one with both young and experienced gymnasts.

Some of the greatest all-round gymnasts in the world have been those who have excelled in performing on the parallel bars.

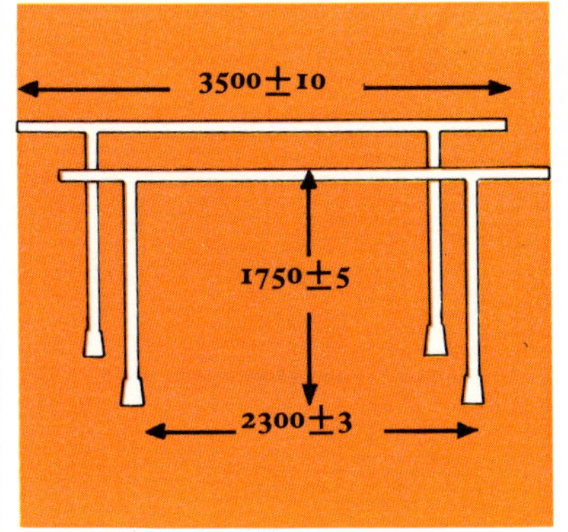

Training

When you begin training on the parallel bars, adjust the bars to a low height. You can also adjust them to a width which will suit you. This width is usually the distance from your elbow to the very end of your stretched finger-tips.

Here are some basic positions for you to practise on the parallel bars. You should practise both as often as you can.

Straight arm support
Upper arm support

In these positions, you can help make your arms and shoulders stronger by performing dips — raising and lowering your body with your arms in the straight arm position or with your shoulders in the upper arm support position.

Straight arm support dips
Upper arm support dips

A simple mount is to jump to a straight arm support. You can also 'walk' along the bars, backwards and forwards, in this position.

Hang support

A third support on the parallel bars is a hang support, such as the one shown here, the inverted piked hang. From here, you can either perform a backwards somersault or thrust your legs forward to bring you up to front support.

Straddle travel

From straight arm support, raise your legs to straddle them over and on the bars. Then place your hands in front of your legs so that you can lean forward and bring your feet up behind you and down into straight arm support again. A related strength move on the parallels is the 'L' support position with legs together inside the supporting arms.

Handstand

The handstand is a vital element of parallel bars work. So it will pay you to practise the handstand first on the floor and then on the end of the bars.

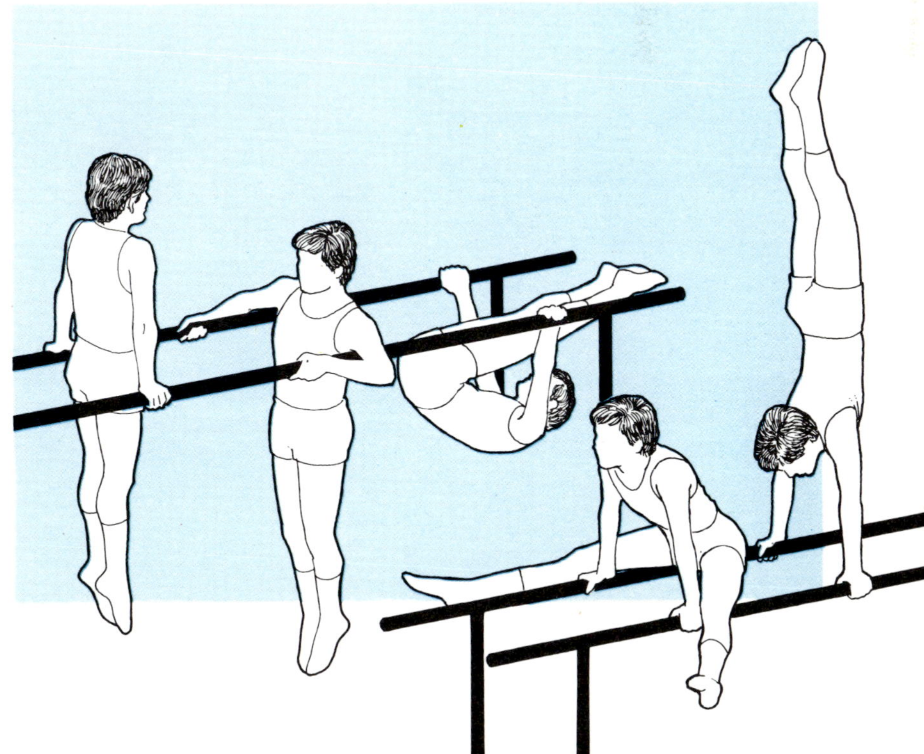

SWING IN STRAIGHT ARM SUPPORT
This is a basic movement in work on the parallel bar. Jump to straight arm support and swing back and forth. First, keep your swings low and easy and then increase their height. It is important to keep your arms locked and swing from the shoulders. On high swings, you can achieve a handstand.

FORWARD SWING UPRISE
Beginners on the parallel bars should also practise the swing in the upper arm support position. Begin the swing with your hips and then swing from your shoulders. When you have gained enough momentum, swing forward to straight arm support.

BACKWARD SWING UPRISE (right)
This is another basic movement and one which is the reverse of the forward swing uprise. In upper arm support, swing forward so that you almost pike your body. Thrusting with your legs, swing back and push on the bars as your body rises behind you. This can take you to straight arm support or to a handstand.

THE KIP (left)
The kip is a long swing forward in the hang position to the inverted pike position. Swing back briefly and then stretch up with your legs, pressing your arms downwards. Correctly executed, the momentum will take you to straight arm support, ready for the next movement.

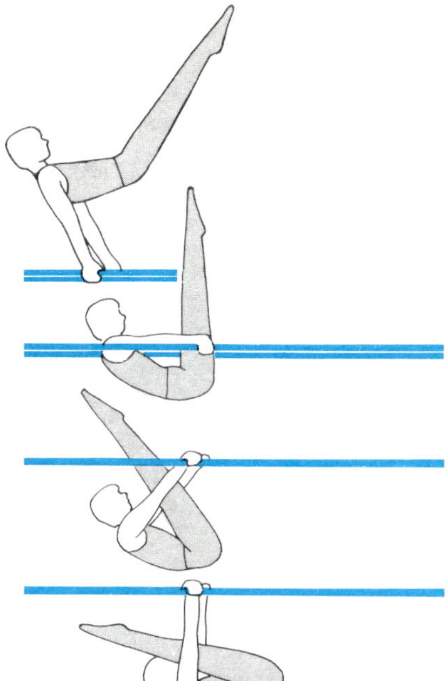

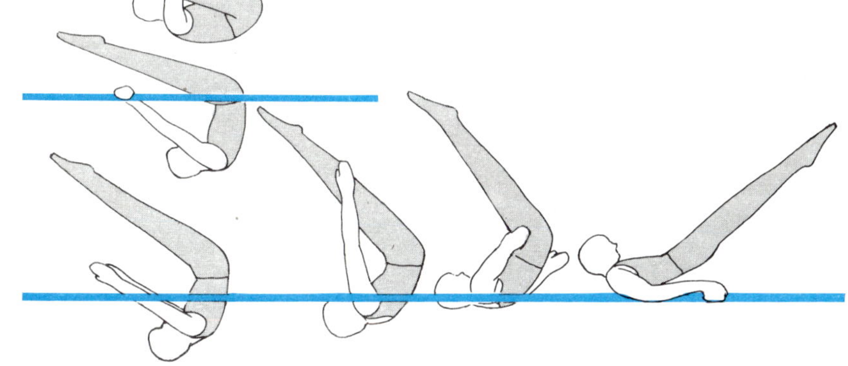

THE CAST (left)

In the cast, you start in straight arm support and swing forwards. Then drop through to the inverted pike position but while you are still swinging forwards, open the pike strongly, pulling on the bars. As your body comes up through the bars, switch your arms to the upper arm support position.

THE STUTZE (right)

In the stutze, you swing forwards from a straight arm support position, perform a half turn and regrasp the bars with both hands. This advanced move can be followed by a handstand or a support position. A stutze with a full turn to handstand is called a Diomidov after the Soviet gymnast who invented it.

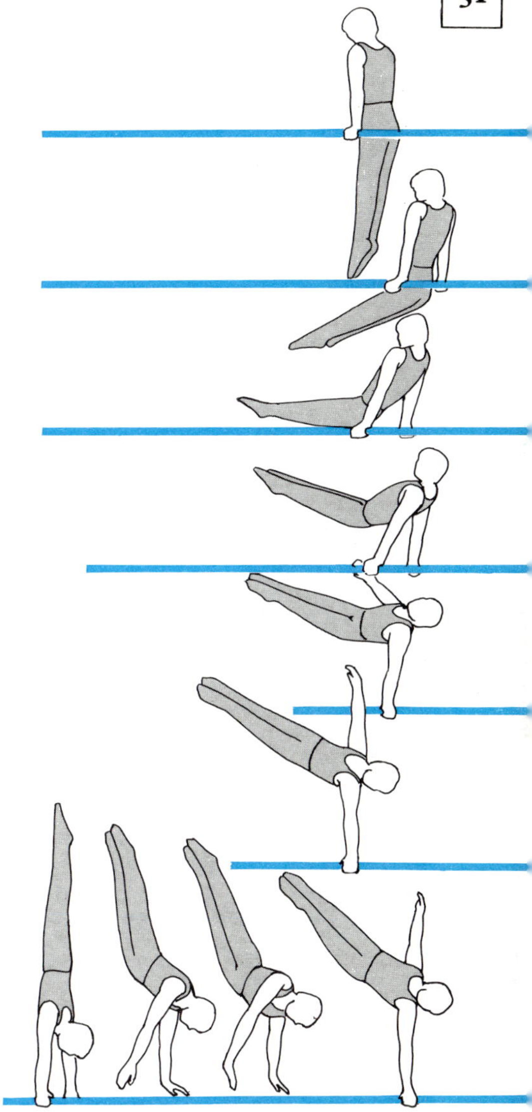

FRONT SOMERSAULT DISMOUNT

In straight arm support, swing back, arching your body and shifting your weight to one side. At the top of the swing, bend your body and push off the bars sideways, straightening out for the landing.

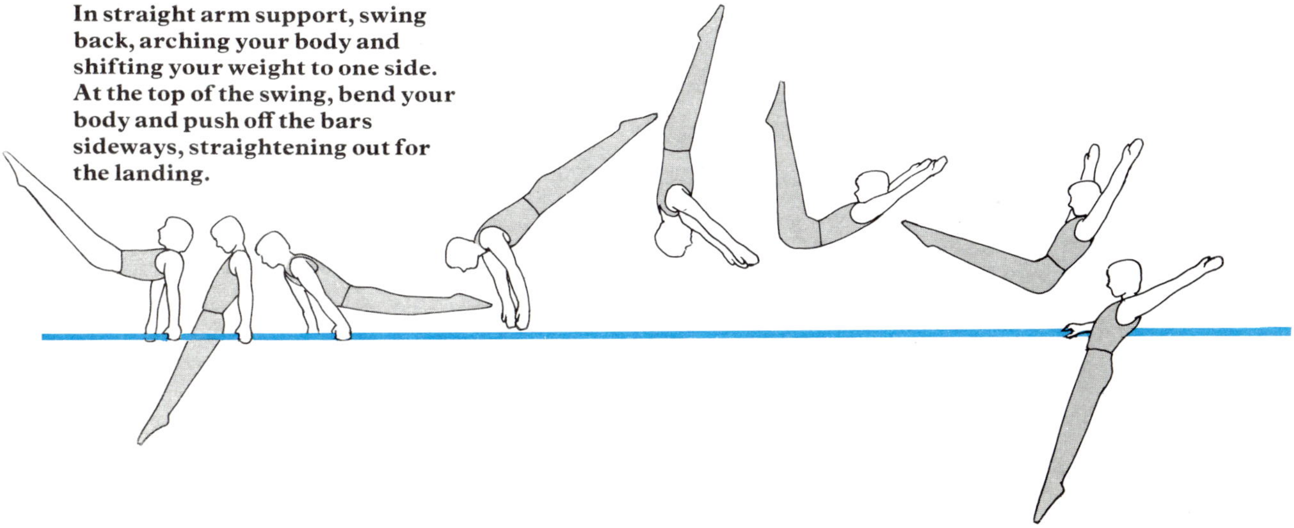

About to regrasp: Tommy Wilson of Great Britain in a reverse somersault on the high bar.

Horizontal bar

The horizontal bar, or high bar as it is usually called, is one of the most spectacular pieces of gymnastics apparatus.

On it, the last event in the men's competition, you must perform continuous swinging movements. These movements must include support turns, wheels or circles, twists and changes of grasp.

During the exercise in a top competition, you also have to release both hands from the bar and regrasp them at the same time.

Through the ages, people have enjoyed swinging from tree branches and travelling tumblers in the Middle Ages found that audiences enjoyed stunts performed on level poles.

The forerunner of the high tensile spring steel bar of today was the thick wooden bar developed by Ludwig Jahn in the 19th century.

This wooden bar was used for strength as well as swinging movements. A century later, the strength-type exercises began to evolve into the modern, swing-based routines.

Although the high bar event is short—about 25 seconds—it contains plenty of thrills for gymnasts and spectators alike.

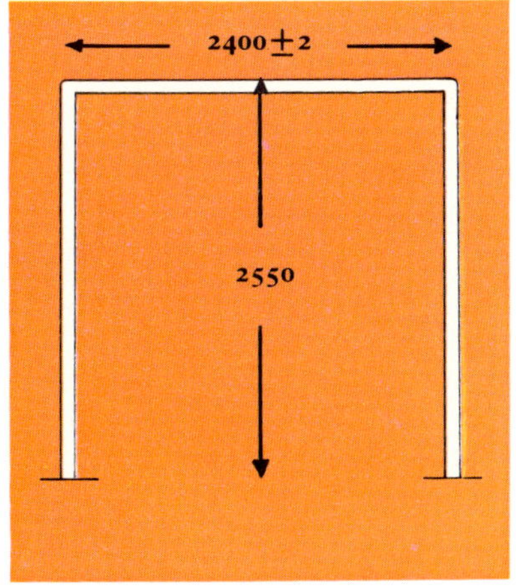

Training

In training for the horizontal bar, remember to look after your hands. Wear handguards and keep the palms of your hands in good condition with daily use of vaseline or hand lotion, as advised in the section on body preparation.

Training sessions should at first be short until your hands have toughened up. Set the bar low, too, for learning basic movements unless you are working in the hang position.

The hang and the support are the two positions through which most movements on the horizontal bar pass.

Hang

Front support

The three grasps used by gymnasts on the horizontal bar are the same as used by girls on the asymmetric bars.

Regular grip

Reverse grip

Mixed grip

You must make sure for safety's sake that you use the right grip according to the direction you travel when making a powerful swing. The rule is: let your thumbs lead in the direction of the swing. This is because the force of the swing could slip your hands from the bar if your fingers did not take most of the strain.

So when you swing forwards, your hands must be in regular grip. When you perform backward swings, then you should use the reverse grip.

The swing

The swing is one of the first movements you should learn on the horizontal bar. Jump to hang and swing forward through your hips. Stretch at the front end of the swing and pike your body slightly when you swing backwards.

As your swings move higher and higher, change the grip of your hands at the end of the swing to suit your direction.

For example, as you swing forward in regular grip, switch to mixed grip and turn your body sideways so that at the peak of the swing you can complete the turn and swing forwards on the return swing with your hands once more in regular grip.

You can build up momentum on the forward swing by pulling up with your hands on the bar as you begin to swing forwards. Pike your legs up in front of you and extend your body at the peak of the swing.

Practise a basic swing, too, in the front support and inverted hang positions, keeping your arms straight.

Back circle

This swing in the front support position can take you around the bar back to front support. Stretch back with your hips, and push away from the bar with straight arms. Now swing your legs down, forwards and then up, body slightly piked, so that you turn under and then over the bar back to your original position.

Horizontal bar

THE KIP

The key to the kip, which takes you from the hang to the front support position, is a powerful forward swing. You must then pike your body and, on the swing back, pull your body to the bar. Let your legs fall forwards as you straighten out. If you swing them behind you, you can start other movements.

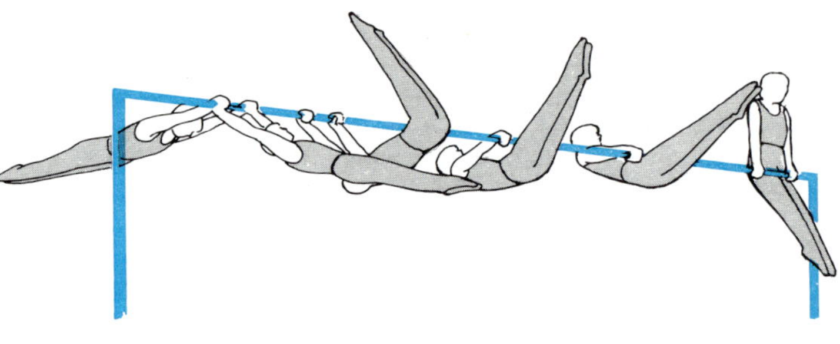

BACKWARDS TURN TO HANDSTAND

This movement requires a strong turn through front support. The momentum of the swing and the pull of your shoulders through straight arms should take you up to handstand. As your body rises, it must be balanced by your legs moving over the bar at an angle before finishing in the upright position.

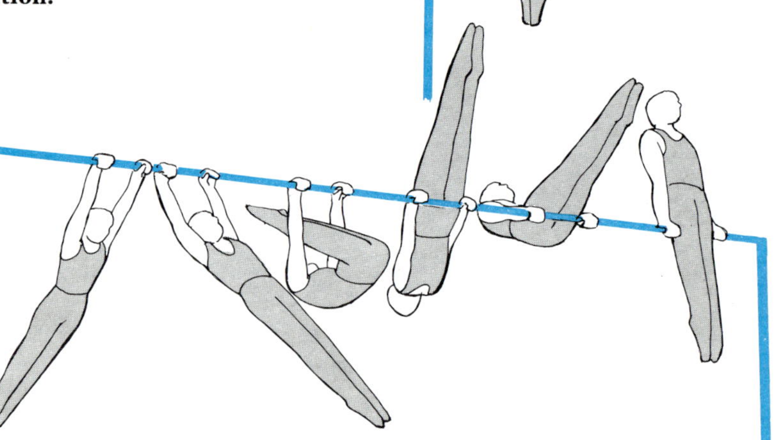

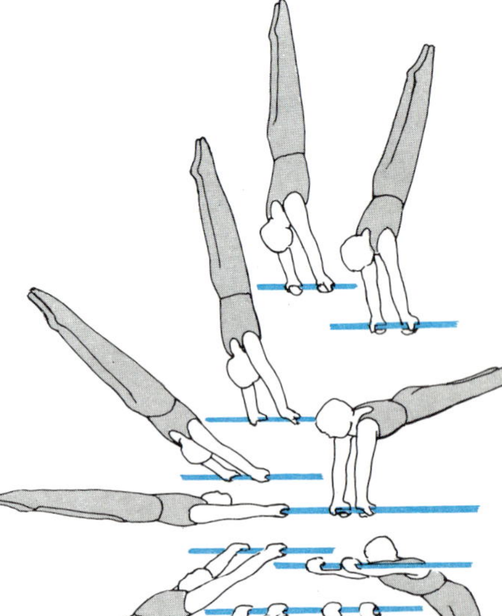

BACK SEAT RISE

At the peak of a forward swing in the hang position, pike to place your legs in the inverted hang position. As you swing backwards, hold the pike position and push against the bar. Then straighten your body when your shoulders begin to rise. Finish in a sitting position on the bar.

GIANT CIRCLE WITH REVERSE GRIP

All leading gymnasts aim to perform this movement. Swing down from a handstand with your body straight. Then arch your back slightly as you rise before bending your hips. At this stage, pull on the high bar so that your shoulders lead you up to handstand again. This should be as smooth as possible.

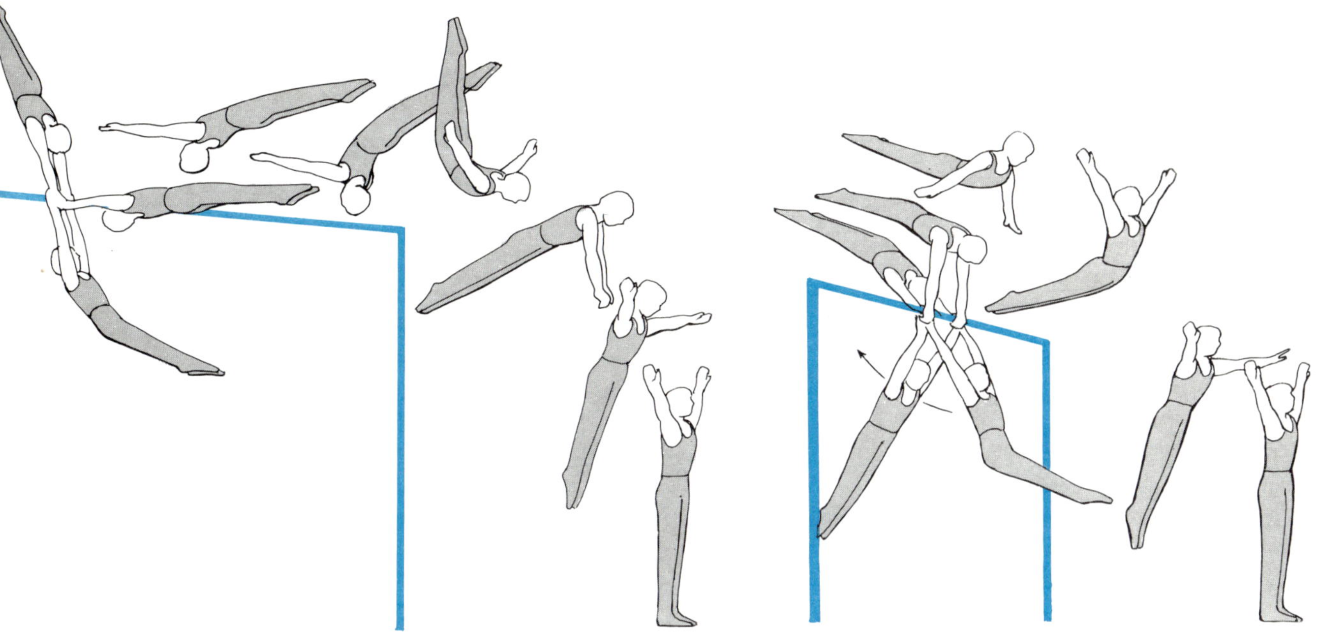

BACKWARDS SOMERSAULT DISMOUNT

The momentum of a forceful forward swing must lift your body up so that when you let go of the bar, you will have enough height to perform a somersault. It can either be one as shown here, or one in the tucked position, or later, as a double with or without a twist according to your experience.

STALDER

The Stalder is named after the Swiss gymnast who first invented it. You circle the bar in the straddle support position moving forwards to a handstand. This movement in reverse is the Endo, first perfected by Yukio Endo, the Japanese gymnast.

HECHT DISMOUNT

This dismount follows the giant circle as shown on the previous page. The swing up to the dismount is performed with a straight body. As you rise above the bar, you push down with your hands to gain extra lift as you 'glide' forward to the landing with arms extended sideways.

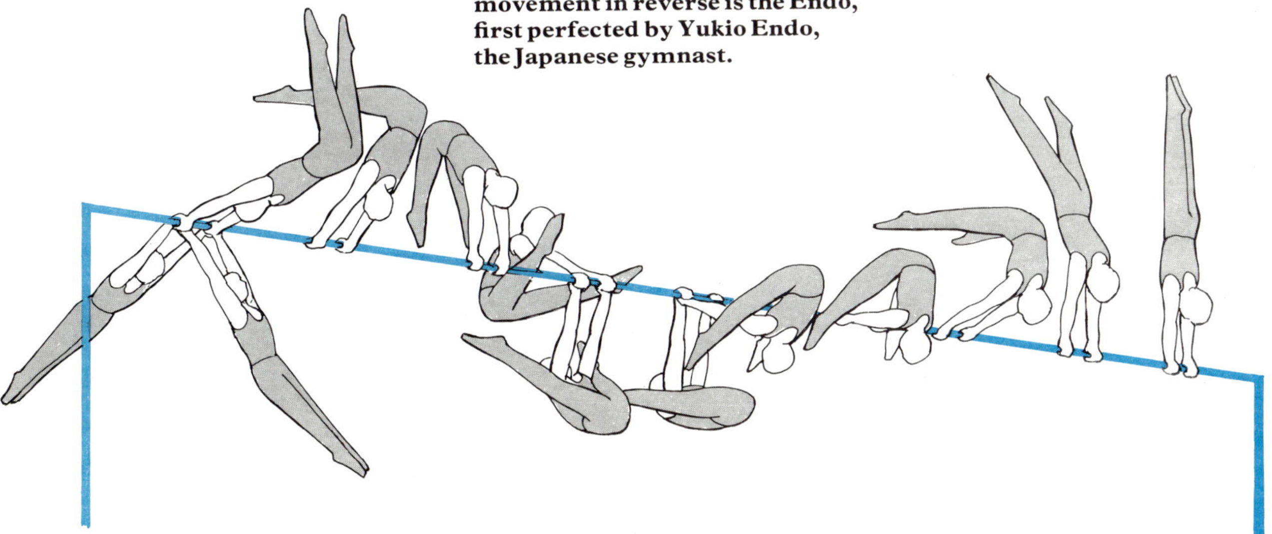

The way to the top

1976 OLYMPIC GAMES

MEN

Team

1 Japan	576.85
2 USSR	576.45
3 GDR (East Germany)	564.65

Combined exercises

1 N. Andrianov (USSR)	116.65
2 S. Kato (Japan)	115.65
3 M. Tsukahara (Japan)	115.575

Floor

1 N. Andrianov (USSR)	19.45
2 V. Marchenko (USSR)	19.425
3 P. Kormann (USA)	19.30

Pommelled horse

1 Z. Magyar (Hungary)	19.70
2 E. Kenmotsu (Japan)	19.575
3 N. Andrianov (USSR)	19.525

Rings

1 N. Andrianov (USSR)	19.65
2 A. Detiatin (USSR)	19.55
3 D. Grecu (Romania)	19.50

Vault

1 N. Andrianov (USSR)	19.45
2 M. Tsukahara (Japan)	19.375
3 H. Kajiyama (Japan)	19.275

Parallel bars

1 S. Kato (Japan)	19.675
2 N. Andrianov (USSR)	19.50
3 M. Tsukahara (Japan)	19.475

High bar

1 M. Tsukahara (Japan)	19.675
2 E. Kenmotsu (Japan)	19.50
3 E. Gienger (FGR)	19.475

WOMEN

Team

1 USSR	390.35
2 Romania	387.15
3 GDR	385.10

Combined exercises

1 N. Comaneci (Romania)	79.275
2 N. Kim (USSR)	78.675
3 L. Tourischeva (USSR)	78.625

Vault

1 N. Kim (USSR)	19.80
2 L. Tourischeva (USSR)	19.65
3 C. Dombek (GDR) (East Germany)	19.65

Asymmetric bars

1 N. Comaneci (Romania)	20.00
2 T. Ungureanu (Romania)	19.80
3 M. Egervari (Hungary)	19.775

Beam

1 N. Comaneci (Romania)	19.95
2 O. Korbut (USSR)	19.725
3 T. Ungureanu (Romania)	19.70

Floor

1 N. Kim (USSR)	19.85
2 L. Tourischeva (USSR)	19.25
3 N. Comaneci (Romania)	19.75

The way to the top

As you will know, the top international competitions in gymnastics are the Olympic Games, the World Championships and the World Cup. There are important regional competitions as well, which include the European Championships, the Pan-American Games and the Asian Games.

The largest competitions such as the World Championships and the Olympic Games have three main parts: a team competition, an individual all-round competition, and individual apparatus finals.

In the last 25 years, two countries have dominated the major team competitions. They are Japan, whose men gymnasts have won every team competition in the Olympic Games and World Championships since 1960, and the Soviet Union whose women have been undefeated with one exception in the team competitions at the same events since 1952. The exception was the 1966 World Championships when Czechoslovakia won.

The greatest star of this period in the individual competitions was undoubtedly Larissa Latynina of the Soviet Union. She won no less than 24 Olympic, world and European gold medals between 1956 and 1964.

Other great names of this time included Vera Caslavska of Czechoslovakia, Miroslav Cerar of Yugoslavia, Boris Shaklin and Yuri Titov of the USSR, and Sawao Kato of Japan.

More recent stars are Mitsuo Tsukahara who invented the vault of his name, Zoltan Magyar of Hungary, Kurt Thomas of the USA, and Ludmila Tourischeva, Nicolai Andrianov and Nelli Kim of the Soviet Union, not forgetting, of course, Olga Korbut and Nadia Comaneci.

Many countries involved in gymnastics hold international

matches against each other and some organise international tournaments to which gymnasts from selected countries are invited. Each country, too, will hold its main championships every year.

If you are a British gymnast, your first competition is likely to be one within your club. Then, as you improve, you can take part in local competitions. If you continue to be successful, your coach or teacher can enter you in an important area competition. And from there you can belong to a squad system at area, regional and national level which provides expert coaching for up-and-coming gymnasts. It is from these squads that future internationals emerge.

Britain also has several national championships which give young gymnasts of talent the chance of becoming even better at the sport. Events of this kind usually receive the support of sponsors.

For example, the *Daily Mirror* newspaper sends two young gymnasts—a boy and a girl—to the Soviet Union on a scholarship every year to train with expert coaches, and Thames Television provides £10,000 a year as training grants through the Junior Gymnast of the Year competition.

If you have the talent and the willpower, there are plenty of chances today for you to start on the way to the top.

WORLD CHAMPIONSHIPS 1978

MEN

Team

1 Japan	579.85
2 USSR	578.90
3 GDR	571.75

Combined exercises

1 N. Andrianov (USSR)	117.20
2 E. Kenmotsu (Japan)	116.55
3 A. Detiatin (USSR)	116.375

Floor

1 K. Thomas (USA)	19.65
2 S. Kasamatsu (Japan)	19.575
3 A. Detiatin (USSR)	19.35

Pommelled horse

1 Z. Magyar (Hungary)	19.80
2 E. Gienger (FGR) (West Germany)	19.425
3 S. Deltchev (Bulgaria)	19.40

Rings

1 N. Andrianov (USSR)	19.70
2 A. Detiatin (USSR)	19.675
3 D. Grecu (Romania)	19.65

Vault

1 J. Shimizu (Japan)	19.60
2 N. Andrianov (USSR)	19.575
3 R. Barthel (GDR)	19.55

Parallel bars

1 E. Kenmotsu (Japan)	19.60
2 =N. Andrianov (USSR)	19.575
2 =H. Kajiyama (Japan)	19.575

High bar

1 S. Kasamatsu (Japan)	19.675
2 E. Gienger (FGR)	19.65
3= G. Kryssin (USSR)	19.60
3= S. Deltchev (Bulgaria)	19.60

WOMEN

Team

1 USSR	388.75
2 Romania	384.25
3 GDR	382.25

Combined exercises

1 E. Moukhina (USSR)	78.725
2 N. Kim (USSR)	78.575
3 N. Shaposhnikova (USSR)	77.875

Vault

1 N. Kim (USSR)	19.625
2 N. Comaneci (Romania)	19.60
3 S. Kraker (GDR)	19.55

Asymmetric bars

1 M. Frederick (USA)	19.80
2 E. Moukhina (USSR)	19.725
3 E. Eberle (Romania)	19.625

Beam

1 N. Comaneci (Romania)	19.625
2 E. Moukhina (USSR)	19.60
3 E. Eberle (Romania)	19.525

Floor

1= N. Kim (USSR)	19.775
1= E. Moukhina (USSR)	19.775
3= E. Eberle (Romania)	19.525
3= K. Johnson (USA)	19.525

Scoring in gymnastics

Scoring in gymnastics

Because scoring in gymnastics depends on the opinion of judges, you may think that sometimes gymnasts could be marked unfairly. While this can happen, of course, the International Gymnastics Federation (FIG) has drawn up strict rules for judges to follow when they judge the exercises performed by gymnasts.

As you will have read, the rules are published in the *Code of Points*. Up to 1948, there were several different systems of scoring, but after the London Olympic Games when there was some confusion over the judging, the FIG decided to create one scoring system for all member countries to use.

So the first *Code of Points* appeared in 1949 and since then has been revised regularly, usually every four years, according to the progress of the sport. Every judge, men's and women's, has to be familiar with the *Code of Points* in order to become qualified.

In important championships and competitions, performances on each piece of apparatus are judged by a panel of four judges with a superior or master judge in charge.

The superior judge gives the gymnast the signal, either by green flag or green light, to begin the exercise. The exercise is then marked out of 10 by the judges who give their marks to the superior judge. The superior judge then crosses off the highest and lowest marks and averages out the two middle marks.

For example, if the four judges produce marks of 9.1, 9.2, 9.3, and 9.4, the superior judge drops 9.1 and 9.4, adds 9.2 and 9.3 and divides the sum by 2, obtaining a result of 9.25 which is the gymnast's score. (What score is arrived at with marks of 9.2, 9.3, 9.4 and 9.5?)

There are limits for differences in judges' marks and the superior judge has to make sure that these limits are observed. The superior judge also marks the gymnast but this mark is only used in a dispute.

The judges are helped by reserve judges who do not mark but act as timekeepers or check that gymnasts work within the limits and areas laid down for the floor and vault.

Gymnasts in top competitions have to perform compulsory or set exercises and voluntary or free exercises. The scoring of these exercises varies for men and women and points can be deducted for general faults as well.

Women's scoring

Women's voluntary exercises, except for the vault, are marked out of 10 in this way:

Difficulty	3.0
Originality and value of connections	1.5
Composition of exercise	0.5
Execution and amplitude	4.0
General impression	1.0
	10.0

Difficulty The *Code of Points* lists movements as either medium

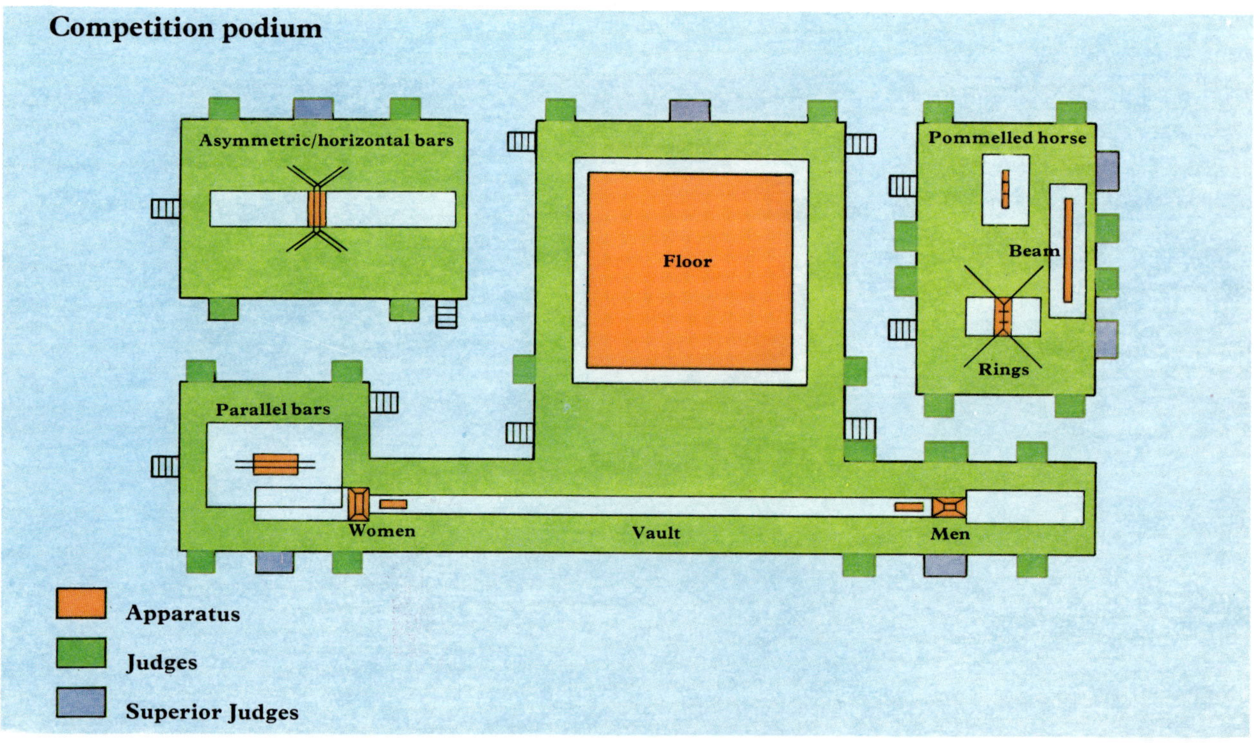

During a competition, the four judges on an apparatus may have to be guided on marking standards by their superior.

difficulties or superior difficulties. A voluntary exercise must contain at least seven difficulties, three of which have to be superior. A superior difficulty is worth 0.6 and a medium one 0.3.

Originality and value of connections This is to encourage you to link movements in ways as interesting as possible.

Composition of exercise The judges mark you on how you have planned your exercise. The more variety of movements you have, the better you will score.

Execution and amplitude Here you are marked for performing each movement of the exercise as fully as possible. Amplitude means the act of being ample.

General impression A gymnast who performs with confidence and grace to the best of her ability will be rewarded here.

Women's compulsory exercises have to follow the description produced for an actual competition and are also marked out of 10, with similar deductions, 0.6 or 0.3, for leaving out superior or medium difficulties. Small changes to compulsory exercises can earn up to 0.2 in deductions.

Men's scoring

In men's voluntary exercises on all apparatus except for the vault, marks are shared as follows:

Difficulty	3.4
Combination	1.6
Execution	4.4
Bonus:	
Risk	0.2
Originality	0.2
Virtuosity	0.2
	10.0

Difficulty Difficulties in men's exercises are set out in the *Code of Points* as three kinds: A (basic) worth 0.2 points, B (medium) 0.4 and C (superior) worth 0.6 points. In major championships, each competition has to have its own fixed amount of these difficulties. The amounts are:

	C	B	A	
Team competition	1	5	4	= 3.4
Individual all-round	2	4	3	= 3.4
Individual apparatus	3	3	2	= 3.4

Combination These points are awarded to the gymnast depending on the skill he shows in combining all the parts into one exercise.

Execution The gymnast earns these points for the accuracy and style of his performance.

Bonus The bonus points are known as R.O.V. and can be earned in the vault as well. The judges evaluate any danger in the exercise, any new moves or expertise and award marks accordingly.

Men's compulsory exercises, as with the women's, have their content decided before the competition. In them, a gymnast can score 9.8 for interpretation and execution, and 0.2 for virtuosity. If you leave out a part, you can lose between 0.1 to 0.5 points. If you add an extra movement, you will have 0.3 deducted with a further penalty of 9.1 to 0.3 if this additional part made the previous or following parts easier.

Entering a competition

Entering a competition
After you have prepared the muscles of your body for gymnastics and learned the basic skills, you will be ready to work towards entering competitions.

Your coach and your club will help you decide what competitions to enter and when. The choice will depend on your progress and your determination.

While success in competitions hinges on how well you have learned your routines, there are also other points to consider that can affect your performances and career in gymnastics. Here are some of these points.

Preparation for a competition
1 Know exactly what exercises—voluntary or compulsory—you are going to perform in the competition including your vault number.
2 Find out when and where the competition is being held and what time you have to arrive.
3 Make sure your entry form is sent in time.
4 Make sure that you have the correct clothing and equipment you need and that it is clean. Do not use any items that could slip or break during your performances.
5 Get a good night's sleep the night before.

Before the event
1 Do not eat anything less than three hours before the competition. Make sure that your last meal is light and can be digested quickly. Avoid fats.
2 Arrive in good time.
3 Find out where you have to report and to whom.
4 Be clean and tidy. Do not smoke.
5 Study the positions of the apparatus and see how much space is available around them, such as the length of the approach run to the vault.
6 Warm up slowly and thoroughly in a track suit.
7 Follow officials' instructions about marching on and off, or about presentation before or after the event.

During the event
1 Be natural. Be respectful. Be confident.
2 Know the rules. For example, girls can lose 0.50 points for leaving the competition area without permission. Boys can have 0.3 deducted for 'undisciplinary and unsportsmanlike behaviour'. Penalties such as these for major competitions can be found in the *Code of Points.*
3 Always present yourself to the superior judge at each apparatus before and after your exercise.
4 Do not become upset by mistakes—yours and other people's—or by delays during the competition.
5 Girls should make sure that their music is ready when needed and that its quality is good—whether taped or played.
6 Bear safety in mind at all times.
7 Perform your best. Enjoy yourself and show it during your performances.

After the event
1 Do not lose your dignity if you have won or lost.
2 Be friendly to your other competitors. You may meet them again at other competitions.
3 Thank the officials. They will have worked hard to make the competition a success.
4 Make a note of mistakes you made in your exercises so that you can improve on them. Also note any exciting moves made by other gymnasts.

Forthcoming competitions
Your club can hear about the important national and area competitions available for young gymnasts through belonging to a regional association of the British Amateur Gymnastics Association, 95 High Street, Slough, Berks. SL1 1DH.

Anyone interested in British gymnastics can become a member of the BAGA or subscribe to *The Gymnast*, the official journal of the BAGA. *The Gymnast* contains news of major competitions and gymnastics personalities the world over.

Useful books
Here are some interesting books for competitive gymnastics:
The World of Gymnastics, ed. Peter Tatlow (Pelham)
Gymnastics for Men, Nik Stuart MBE (Stanley Paul)
Women's Gymnastics, Jill Coulton (EP)
Your Book of Gymnastics, Pauline and Jim Prestidge (Faber and Faber)
Gymnastics Safety Manual, ed. Eugene Wettstone (Pennsylvania State University Press)

Finally, remember again that you can reach the top in gymnastics through nothing but hard, hard work.

If you do succeed, however, your success will be all the more satisfying because you will have overcome your greatest opponent.

Yourself.

Called the 'Black Panther' by British sports writers, Elvira Saadi of the Soviet Union was one of the most exciting international competitors on floor during the mid '70s.

Glossary

A, B, C parts Ratings of difficulty in men's movements. A is basic, B medium and C is superior.
Amplitude Fullest possible extent of movement and a standard of judging in women's gymnastics.
Arabesque A balance pose for women on beam and floor with the body supported on one leg, the other leg stretched back, one arm stretched to the side and the other stretched up.
Arab spring See round-off.
Back flip A back handspring. Also called a flic-flac.
B.A.G.A. British Amateur Gymnastics Association, the controlling body of gymnastics in Britain.
Barani Version of aerial cartwheel or beam dismount performed without hands.
Body tension The control of muscles in, for example, the back and thighs to prevent the body from flexing during a movement.

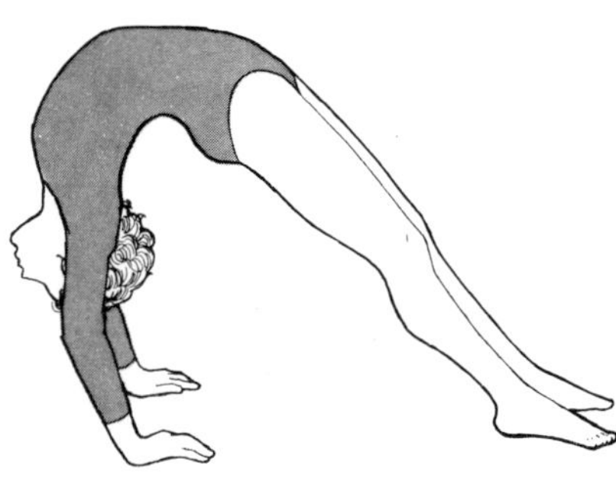

Bridge The firm arch of the body when the feet come to the floor from a handstand, falling backwards with knees bent.
Cartwheel Sideways rotation of the body from feet to feet moving vertically through the hands.
Code of Points Book published by the International Gymnastics Federation (FIG) with rules for judging gymnasts.
Cross Also crucifix. Strength move on the rings in which the gymnast's arms are extended horizontally with his body vertical.
Croup Part of the long horse nearest the vaulter or the part of the pommelled horse to the right of the gymnast.
Diomidov A movement on the parallel bars in which the gymnast swings forward and makes a full turn to handstand.
Dislocation Grip on the bars or rings in which the gymnast hangs with arms behind the back.
Dismount The final movement in an exercise when the gymnast jumps down from the apparatus.
Element A movement in an exercise.
F.I.G. Féderation Internationale de Gymnastique, the International Gymnastics Federation which is the world governing body of gymnastics.
Giant circle Swing or wheel in which the gymnast circles the high bar with arms and body extended.
Handguards Straps which protect the palms of the hand during performances when the body is in support on certain apparatus, i.e. asymmetric bars, pommelled horse, rings, parallel bars and high bar. Usually made of leather, lamp wick or synthetic materials.
Handspring A leap onto the hands followed by a thrust in the same direction on to the feet again.
Hang A basic position where a gymnast hangs below a bar or rings.
Hecht A dismount from bars and a vault in which the gymnast extends the arms sideways, body nearly horizontal before landing.
Hip circle A circle around a bar with the hips held close to the bar.
Inverted hang Here the gymnast hangs vertically upside down on the rings.
Kip Also upstart. A movement which raises a gymnast from a hang to a support position on a bar or rings.

The beginning of a mill circle. The gymnast is about to fall forward; look at her grasp.

Layout When the gymnast's body is held straight and extended in vaulting, swinging or somersaulting.

Mill circle A circle of a bar with the legs astride over the bar.
Mixed grip A grip on a bar by both hands in which one palm faces the gymnast while the other faces away.
Mount Move by which a gymnast jumps on to an apparatus at the beginning of an exercise.
Neck Part of the long horse furthest from the vaulter or the part of the pommelled horse to the left of the gymnast.
Pike A position in which the gymnast is folded or bent at the hips, keeping the legs straight.
Pirouette Full turn of the body when in a standing position.
Planche A strength move by which the gymnast holds his body horizontal supported by his arms and hands alone.
Podium The raised platform or platforms on which a major competition takes place.
Radochla A movement on the asymmetric bars consisting of a somersault between the bars.
Regular grip The grip by both hands on a bar with the palms facing away from the body.
Reverse grip The opposite to the regular grip on a bar. The palms of the hands face the gymnast.
Round-off Also Arab spring. Like the cartwheel except that the legs come together when they reach the vertical and the gymnast makes a quarter turn to land facing the direction of approach.
Routine The planned order of movements which make up an exercise.
R.O.V. Risk, originality and virtuosity are qualities in men's exercises which earn bonus points of 0.2 points each.
Saddle Centre part of the pommelled horse.
Salto A complete somersault from feet to feet or performed on apparatus.
Scale A balance pose held by the gymnast on one leg.
Sole circle A turn around a bar with both hands and feet on the bar.
Splits Describing a movement, leap or pose in which the legs are extended in a straight line, usually level with the floor. Splits can be sideways or with either leg forwards.

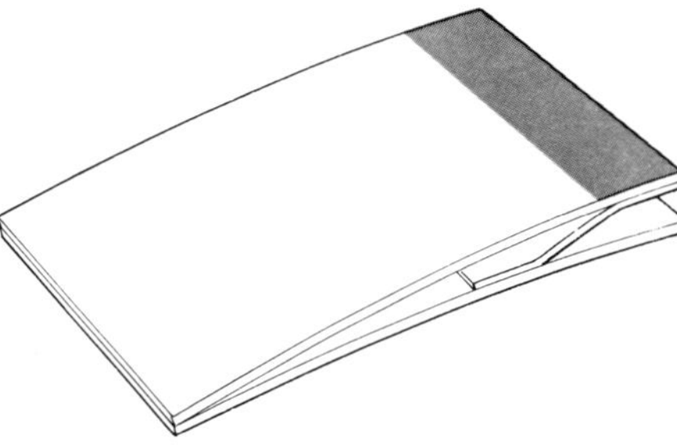

Springboard Equipment used with apparatus to give gymnasts greater height in vaulting or on mounting apparatus.
Stag A leap or pose with one leg bent and the other held straight back.
Stalder A backwards circling movement on the high bar in straddle support to handstand.
Stoop Vault so named because the gymnast 'stoops' or leans forward when over the horse.
Straddle Movement with the legs held straight and apart.
Strelli A backward roll on the parallel bars leading to a handstand.
Stutze A movement on the parallel bars when the gymnast makes a half turn as he swings forward in straight arm support.
Support In this position, the body is supported by straight arms with the hands below the shoulders. This is a basic position in gymnastics.
Tinsica This movement resembles a cartwheel with the arms and upper body, and a walkover with the legs.
Tsukahara A vault named after the Japanese gymnast who invented it. It consists of a cartwheel onto the horse and a one-and-a-half somersault off to land.
Trampette Small version of trampoline; used in training or gymnastics displays.
Tuck Position in somersaulting when the knees are bent up to the chest.
Uprise A swinging movement which takes a gymnast from hang to support on apparatus.
Upstart See kip.
Walkover A movement through a handstand from feet to feet, forwards or backwards, with legs leading each other.
Yamashita A handspring vault with the body piking before landing. Named after the Japanese gymnast who first performed it.

Index

Credits

Photographs
Alan Burrows
Peter Moeller

Artwork
Colin Ede
Michael Bilsland